Stop Negative Thinking

The ultimate self-help guide to stop worrying, control your thoughts, and develop a positive mindset. Become a happy person again building new habits

© Copyright 2019 - All rights reserved.

The content contained within this book may not be reproduced, duplicated or transmitted without direct written permission from the author or the publisher.

Under no circumstances will any blame or legal responsibility be held against the publisher, or author, for any damages, reparation, or monetary loss due to the information contained within this book, either directly or indirectly.

Legal Notice:
This book is copyright protected. It is only for personal use. You cannot amend, distribute, sell, use, quote or paraphrase any part, or the content within this book, without the consent of the author or publisher.

Disclaimer Notice:
Please note the information contained within this document is for educational and entertainment purposes only. All effort has been executed to present accurate, up to date, reliable, complete information. No warranties of any kind are declared or implied. Readers acknowledge that the author is not engaging in the rendering of legal, financial, medical or professional advice. The content within this book has been derived from various sources. Please consult a licensed professional before attempting any techniques outlined in this book.

By reading this document, the reader agrees that under no circumstances is the author responsible for any losses, direct or indirect, that are incurred as a result of the use of information contained within this document, including, but not limited to, errors, omissions, or inaccuracies.

Table of Contents

Introduction 1

Chapter 1: Why Am I So Negative? 7
- **What is Negative Thinking?** 7
  - Guilty Thinking 9
  - Shoulding 10
  - All-or-Nothing Thinking 10
  - Worst Case Scenario Thinking/Worrying 11
  - Predicting the Future 12
  - Mind Reading 13
  - Blaming 13
  - Comparing 14
  - Pessimism 15
- **What Causes Negative Thinking?** 15
- **What Are the Effects of Negative Thinking?** 18
- **How Can I Silence Those Negative Thoughts?** 21

Chapter 2: Why Do I Worry So Much? 25
- **Harmful vs. Normal Worry** 26
- **How Can I Stop Worrying?** 29
  - The Cycle of Worry 29
  - Question Your Worries 30
  - Remember Past Successes 34
  - Put Worry on Your Schedule 35
  - Reach Out for Help 35
  - Practice, Practice, Practice 36

Chapter 3: Why Am I So Hard on Myself? 39
- **Where Does Negative Self-Talk Come From?** 39
- **How Can I Stop Negative Self-Talk?** 42
  - Question Your Thoughts 42
  - Change What You Can 44
  - Release Judgment of Your Thoughts 45

Use Positive Affirmations 46
List Your Positive Qualities 47
Ask for Help 48

Chapter 4: How Can I Control My Thoughts? 51
How to Control Your Mind 53
Become the Conscious Observer of Your Thoughts 53
Awareness 54
Perform a Brain-Dump...55
Get Out of Your Head and into Your Body 58
Become Emotionally Strong 61

Benefits of a Thoughts Journal 65
Journal Tip #1: Try to Write Every day 65
Journal Tip #2: Carry Your Journal with You...........................66
Journal Tip #3: You Don't Have to Be a Writer 66
Journal Tip #4: Your Journal, Your Rules 67

The Power of Sleep 67
How to Get Proper Sleep?... 71

Chapter 5: How Can I Start Thinking Positively?....... 77
Life Has Two Faces...81

Discovering New Good Habits 83
The Good Habits, The Bad Habits, and The Ugly Negativity.....87
In Hindsight.. 89
The Difficulty of Creating Good Habits 91
Sticking to Good Habits 93
Positive Habits Require Positive Thinking.................................99

The Power of Positive Thinking 100
Tip #1: Start Your Day with Affirmations.................................102
Tip #2: Think About the Good Things, No Matter How Small They Are...103
Tip #3: Crank Up Your Humor 103
Tip #4: Failures Are Lessons 104
Tip #5: Watch Out for Negative Self-Talk 104
Focus on the Present 106
Have a Positive Circle of Friends..107

Effects of Positivity on Health 108
Becoming Happier 111
    Happiness Tip #1: Find Ways to Feel Better About Yourself ... 111
    Happiness Tip #2: Create Balance 112
    Happiness Tip #3: Make Positive Memories 113
    Happiness Tip #4: Be Kind and Generous 114
    Happiness Tip #5: Make Offline Connections 114
    Happiness Tip #6: Spend Smart 115
    Happiness Tip #7: Engage with Negativity 116
    Happiness Tip #8: Identify and Live Your Values 116
    Happiness Tip #9: Set Achievable Goals 117
    Happiness Tip #10: Speak Up 117
    Happiness Tip #11: Be Accountable 117
Conclusion 119
References 123

Introduction

"I have the worst luck."

"Things just never work out for me."

"Mondays stink. I hate this job."

"I can't believe I embarrassed myself in front of all those people. I'm such a klutz."

"I'll always be broke. It's too hard to make a good living."

"My friend hasn't responded to my text message; she must be mad at me."

"Another headache? Something must be really wrong with me."

"My spouse is such a slob; I'm the only one who ever cleans up around here."

"I should have gone to the gym yesterday. I'll never lose this weight."

"Oh great, it's raining. Now my day off is ruined."

Do these sentences sound familiar, like you are getting a glimpse into your own brain? You are not alone. Every person on the planet struggles with negative thoughts from time to time. It is merely part of the human experience. A miserable night's sleep, an argument with a loved one, an unexpected piece of bad news, even just waking up on the wrong side of the bed—all these things and more, can make it hard to look on the bright side sometimes.

In other words, negative thoughts are normal, and they are pretty harmless as long as they pass through our minds quickly. They can sometimes be a boon, in fact, opening our eyes to situations or behaviors that we want to change. For example, if you find yourself grumpy about the fact that your friend was late yet again, it might motivate you to communicate with them openly about your feelings. In this case, your negative thoughts could help you resolve a problematic situation and ultimately strengthen your friendship.

However, if negative thoughts like the ones above run on a constant loop through your mind day in and day out, you may have become caught in a pattern of negative thinking. When you are in such a mode, your mind will be consumed with worry or anxiety over what might go wrong in the future, and guilt or resentment over what went wrong in the past. Over time, this constant focus on the negative can impact your relationships, health, productivity, and overall life outlook and satisfaction.

Like any habit, a pattern of negative thinking can be hard to break. Picture your thoughts as a bicycle that you ride around the track of your mind. If you ride along the same route every single day, eventually, you will create a groove in the path. It will take more effort to ride your bike along any other route, and you will find yourself naturally falling back into that groove. This is what constant negative thinking does; it creates a rut of negativity in your mind. As time goes on, negativity becomes your default, the groove in which you naturally ride your mental bike, and it will be harder and harder to break free and find the good in any situation.

Negative thoughts can become a pattern, but like all patterns, you can break out of it. That was the bad news. The good news is that just like any habit, you can break your pattern of negative thinking. While it will not happen overnight, you can take steps to help cover over that old negative rut in your mind and create a new, more positive route. In fact, You have taken the first step just by picking up this book.

Here is another piece of good news; you are not alone in your constant negative thinking. Many people suffer from similar negative patterns. Why is this good news? Since negative thinking affects so many people and can cause pain and suffering, countless experts, from mental health professionals to spiritual teachers, have poured extensive time and research into uncovering ways to help people put an end to the unfavorable mental loop. Once you decide to break out of old patterns, you will have an array of practices and strategies to draw on, including those found in the following chapters. The information, tips, and tricks collected in these pages will help you to better recognize your negative thought patterns and triggers, catch yourself more quickly when you begin to spiral into negative thinking, and use simple, clear practices to shift your mindset toward the positive.

This book is not intended to diagnose or treat clinical mental health issues such as depression or anxiety disorders, although negative thinking certainly plays a role in these conditions, and the practices discussed here may also be useful for people living with mental health issues. Instead, this book is geared towards the more ubiquitous, garden-variety negativity and worry that afflicts so many in today's competitive, busy, always connected society.

If you find yourself waking up on the wrong side of the bed more often than not . . . If you beat yourself up for every little mistake . . . If your critical or demanding attitude is hurting your relationship with your friends and family . . . If your need for perfection from yourself and others is killing your productivity and your relationships at work . . . If you are lying awake worrying night after night . . . If you have been feeling "stuck" and simply want to experience more joy and pleasure in your day-to-day life—then this book was written with you in mind.

Chapter 1: Why Am I So Negative?

What is Negative Thinking?

It was already mentioned in the introduction but it bears repeating: negative thoughts are normal. We cannot escape the occasional low mood, worry, or gloomy thought. In fact, trying to ban all negativity from our lives just creates more negative stress because it puts unrealistic pressure on ourselves. It's perfectly natural to experience worry if you suddenly lose your job or to feel annoyed if your neighbors keep throwing loud parties late into the night. It's when you begin to fixate solely on these thoughts and feelings that they become a problem. In the context of this book, the phrase "negative thinking" doesn't refer to occasional passing thoughts or worry over one-off stressful situations, but rather to the habit of repetitive, persistent, pervasive negative thinking. This could come in the form of constantly replaying past events or conversations, overanalyzing, beating yourself up, fixating on a situation, or worrying obsessively about the future. People struggling with this habit might think negatively about themselves, others, or the world around them in general. Whatever form their negative thoughts take, however, eventually the habit will begin to seriously impact their lives.

Negative thinking can be sneaky as well. It can creep up on you without you really noticing it until suddenly, negative thoughts hold sway over your day or even your life. After all, no one sets out to develop a bad habit; it happens gradually over time and in subtle ways. We often get so caught up in our day-to-day lives that we rarely take the time to stop and really look at our thoughts. As a result, it is easy to engage in repetitive negative thinking without even realizing it. You might just notice that you're in a bad mood or that you feel "off" but upon closer examination, you realize that you've been mentally rehashing a recent fight with your mother all day. Learning to catch yourself as soon as you start to get caught up in a negative thought or story so that you can stop the momentum is just one of the strategies you'll learn in later chapters.

There are a few types of negative thinking that commonly show up in people's lives, and they often overlap. These include: guilty thinking, "shoulding," all-or-nothing thinking, worst case scenario thinking, predicting the future, mind reading, blaming, comparing, and overall pessimism.

Guilty Thinking

When a person is caught up in guilty thinking, they often find themselves trapped in the past. They feel guilty for mistakes they have made, replaying them over and over again. Perhaps you said something in anger that hurt your spouse's feelings; while it's normal to feel remorse in this situation, a habitual negative thinker will continue to beat themselves up for their words and feel crippling guilt even after they've apologized to their spouse. Another common example is making a mistake at work. Perhaps you input an incorrect number on a report, resulting in embarrassment in front of your boss or in extra work needed from yourself or your colleagues to fix the error. We all make mistakes, but negative thinkers will be unable to let it go. They'll replay it over and over, beating themselves up and telling themselves things like, "I can't believe I didn't double-check those numbers. I'm such an idiot. I should never have volunteered to write that report. That meeting was so embarrassing, I looked like an incompetent screw-up. Heck, maybe I am!"

Guilty thinking often goes hand-in-hand with "shoulding" all-or-nothing thinking, and predicting the future.

Shoulding

This line of negative thinking happens when a person obsesses over what they "should" or "should not" do. In the previous example about the error at work, the person slipped into "should" thinking by telling themselves that they should have been more careful or that they should not have volunteered for the job. Perhaps you have been unhappy with your physical fitness and find yourself constantly thinking, "I shouldn't have eaten that. I should have gone to the gym today." While setting goals is admirable and important for our continued personal growth, constantly lecturing ourselves for things we have or have not done—or "shoulding on ourselves", in the words of motivational speaker Loretta Laroche (Laroche, 2008)—can be counterproductive to those goals. Instead of inspiring and motivating us, it just makes us feel worse about ourselves.

Should thinking often overlaps with guilty thinking, predicting the future, and mind reading.

All-or-Nothing Thinking

Always. Never. Every time. A person who finds themselves using words like these on a regular basis may be caught up in all-or-nothing thinking. If you are an all-or-nothing thinker, you see the world in black and white. Things are either good or bad. A certain aspect of your life always goes well or goes horribly. You are either perfect at something or a failure. So, how is this line of thinking negative? It leaves no room for normal human error or for happenstance. Say you are single and go out on a first date that doesn't go very well. If you are an all-or-nothing thinker, you might tell yourself, "I always screw up dating so why even bother trying? Relationships just never work out for me." Similarly, if you have a bad experience at a restaurant, you might think, "You can never find good customer service anymore. Society is just failing." This line of thinking ultimately lowers your level of regard for yourself and for the people around you.

All-or-nothing thinking often relates to worst case scenario thinking, predicting the future, and overall pessimism.

Worst Case Scenario Thinking/Worrying

Otherwise known as "catastrophizing" (Grohol, 2018), worst case scenario thinking or worrying happens when we believe in the worst possible outcome for a given situation. Recall our earlier example of an error at work. If you engage in worst case scenario thinking, you might worry and think, "I can't believe I made such a stupid mistake. I'm obviously going to get fired now." Perhaps you have a splitting headache and immediately think, "It must be a brain tumor." Similarly, perhaps a loved one is a bit late in contacting you and you start thinking, "There must have been a terrible accident." Clearly, such thinking can induce severe worry or even anxiety, particularly if it's a constant pattern.

Worst case scenario thinking often goes hand-in-hand with all-or-nothing thinking, predicting the future, and mind reading.

Predicting the Future

This line of negative thinking is very similar to worst case scenario thinking but it relates specifically to events and situations in the future. If you engage in this type of negative thinking, you view the potential for future happiness or success as very low. We could also call this "why bother" thinking. Imagine you line up an interview for your dream job; if you are caught in a pattern of predicting the future negatively, you might think, "I know I'm just going to be awkward and screw it up. Why should I even bother going?" Predicting-the-future thinking can influence your relationships as well. Perhaps you have moved to a new city and are invited to a party; your negative thought pattern might have you believe that people won't like you so you shouldn't attend.

Predicting the future thinking relates closely to worst case scenario thinking, all-or-nothing thinking, and overall pessimism. The future is always uncertain. Giving it certainty is only going to cause you mental anguish.

Mind Reading

When you engage in mind reading, you believe that you know what other people are thinking. You make assumptions about people's beliefs, thoughts, and feelings—and those assumptions are typically negative. You might walk by a group of co-workers and hear them laughing and think that they must be talking about you. If a friend doesn't respond to your text message immediately, you might jump to the conclusion that she must be angry with you. This line of thinking can be particularly harmful for your relationships because it makes you automatically assume the worst about people.

Mind reading often goes hand-in-hand with predicting the future and worst case scenario thinking.

Blaming

Blaming comes in two varieties: self-blame and blame of others. People who self-blame feel that they are responsible for everything that goes wrong in their lives. From their company not landing a prospective client to a special dinner not turning out well to missing an appointment because of traffic, they will believe that it was all their fault. Holding yourself accountable and taking responsibility for your actions and behaviors is healthy, but self-blame takes this to an unhealthy level, leading to low self-esteem and feelings of failure. When people perpetually place the blame on others, on the other hand, they abdicate their responsibility for any role they might have played. Someone who blames others might complain about their overly chatty coworker who prevents them from getting their work done rather than taking responsibility for their own lack of productivity. Similarly, they might choose to complain daily about how other drivers make their commute so long rather than just accepting the reality that everyone is sitting in the same traffic. Blaming can negatively impact your relationships, as well as diminish your sense of control over your own life and your ability to accept life as it is.

Blaming goes hand-in-hand with all-or-nothing thinking and pessimism.

Comparing

Comparing ourselves to others and finding ourselves lacking is a very common form of negative thinking. Virtually everyone has experienced instances when their inner critic has piped up. People might compare their looks, their relationship status, their wealth, their career path, or their material belongings. They also might compare themselves to their friends and family or to complete strangers. Constant comparison can lead to an overall feeling of dissatisfaction with your life and lowered self-esteem.

Comparing often goes along with worst case scenario thinking and predicting the future.

Pessimism

This is too good to last. Life is just supposed to be hard. People can't be trusted. Nothing is certain but death and taxes. If you find yourself making statements like these often, you might be engaging in overall pessimistic thinking. When you have this mindset, you expect things to go poorly. You expect other people and yourself to let you down. You find it hard to accept or trust when good things happen. Some people who are deeply caught in pessimistic thinking can even begin to take pleasure in situations going awry because it validates their worldview.

Pessimism relates closely to worst case scenario thinking, predicting the future, and blaming.

What Causes Negative Thinking?

Have you ever wondered, "Why am I so negative?" Or perhaps a loved one has told you, "You need to look on the bright side more often." Where does negative thinking stem from? Why do some people look at life as a glass half full while others see it as half empty? Is it nature or nurture?

It's become a commonly accepted idea that we are born with our own natural happiness set point. This is the level of happiness that we experience regardless of what is happening in our lives; whether everything is going well or we are experiencing challenges, our happiness set point remains generally the same. In fact, it's been shown that even when people experience a significant positive event like winning the lottery or a significant negative event like a serious medical diagnosis, their happiness set point returns to its baseline after about a year (Bloom, 2017). If people have happiness set points, it stands to reason that we also have our own individual levels of positivity and negativity. So, it may be the case that some people are just more predisposed to negative thinking than others. This is the nature side of the coin.

Our early childhood experiences also impact our personalities, mindsets, and worldviews. If you were raised in a household where negative thinking was prevalent, you likely learned some of the same behaviors. Perhaps you had an overly critical parent, causing you to compare and judge yourself harshly later in life. A parent who frequently expressed pessimistic thoughts may have taught you that the world is harsh or that the cards are stacked against you. More traumatic childhood experiences, such as neglect or abandonment, can lead to negative thinking patterns as well. Someone who suffered early trauma may engage in worst case scenario thinking, finding it hard to trust other people or take their word. Clearly, nurture plays as large a part as nature in determining whether you will be plagued by negative thinking.

A pattern of negative thinking can also be caused by stressful life events beyond childhood. The end of a relationship, the loss of a job, or a health scare can all spark negative thoughts which if not addressed can soon spiral out of control into habitual pessimistic thinking. Negative thinking functions like a feedback loop: the more we focus our attention on what's going wrong in our lives or in the world, the worse we feel. And the worse we feel, the harder it will be to have a positive attitude. It becomes a vicious cycle and those grooves of negativity in our mental track just get deeper and deeper.

For some people, negative thinking can even develop into an addiction. People for whom negativity becomes an addiction derive a sort of pleasure from the habit. As mentioned earlier, pessimistic thoughts can be used as a way to validate a person's worldview. Similarly, negative thoughts can be used to cement a person's identity ("I'm always a victim") or to try to make sense of or control the world around them ("People are just bad, that's all there is to it.") (Colier, 2019).

So much for how the habit of negative thinking can develop. Where do the specific negative thoughts themselves come from? If you begin to pay attention to the content of your negative thoughts, you'll notice that they fall into one of two camps: anxiety or fear about the future or guilt or anger about the past. We all experience these feelings from time to time, but habitual negative thinkers dwell on the past or the future and find it hard or even impossible to let their thoughts go and focus on the present.

For many people, negative thinking crops up in specific situations or with specific people. You may experience negative thinking in the form of social anxiety. Perhaps you worry that people won't like you or are talking about you behind your back in social settings; you might also find yourself constantly comparing yourself to others or judging them harshly. Some people are plagued by negative thinking in their work environments; they might complain constantly about their boss, their coworkers, or their customers, or demand perfection from themselves and others. Negativity can crop up at home as well. Perhaps you find yourself constantly criticizing your family members; you might also be consumed with worry about the health and well-being of your family or feel like you need to "do it all" yourself and thus make yourself a martyr. Your negativity could center on your body image and looks, your finances, or politics and the general state of the world.

What Are the Effects of Negative Thinking?

Breaking a habit like negative thinking is hard, but truly comprehending the impact of habitual negative thinking can give you the motivation to make a change. You might not even realize all the ways in which constant negative thoughts are intruding on your life.

One major effect is fairly obvious right off the bat: negative thinking creates negative feelings. People who constantly think gloomy thoughts will often feel irritable, sad, angry, hopeless, anxious, or apathetic. Habitual negative thinking can even develop into a more serious mental health condition such as depression or anxiety disorder. The bottom line is that thinking gloomy thoughts makes you feel bad.

Constant negativity can take a toll on your physical health as well. For example, constant worrying can disrupt your sleep and keep you up at night, leaving you feeling drained of energy and unable to concentrate. When you are tired and lethargic, you might be less likely to exercise or make healthy food choices. The stress produced by constant negative thinking can also drive people to unhealthy coping mechanisms such as smoking cigarettes or drinking alcohol in excess. And the list of physical effects doesn't end there. Perpetual anxiety or anger can increase your blood pressure and impact your digestion. Constant stress, such as that brought on by worry and negativity, raises the levels of cortisol produced in the body; this in turn can lower your immune system's ability to fight off infections. Studies have even found that pessimism, cynicism, and depression can increase a person's chances of heart disease and stroke (Hoffman, 2015).

In addition to eroding both your mental and your physical health, perpetual negative thinking affects your life in many other ways as well. While it might not seem obvious, one area of your life that can be impacted by negative thinking is your finances. The feelings of sadness, hopelessness, or depression brought on by negative thinking might make it hard for you to focus at work, thus reducing your productivity and eventually even threatening your job security. Similarly, negative self-judgments could keep you stuck in menial or low-paying work and make you less likely to apply for more lucrative employment opportunities. Some people turn to shopping as a way to distract themselves from negative thoughts and make themselves feel better; this can lead to overspending or even a shopping addiction.

Over time, negative thinking patterns can damage relationships as well. Most people won't want to spend time with someone who constantly complains, criticizes, or belittles others. In fact, research suggests that just listening to another person complaining can actually have negative health impacts; the brain of the person listening releases stress hormones that can reduce cognitive functions and lead to overall greater levels of stress (Montenegro, 2015). If you are a perpetual negative thinker, you may find friends or romantic partners begin to pull away from you. Similarly, you might have trouble making new friends. Work relationships can also be challenged by constant negativity; your colleagues may be hesitant to involve you in group work or to help you out with a project. Being labeled as difficult at work can even threaten your job itself.

A negative mindset can prevent you from solving problems effectively. This might sound counterintuitive: after all, shouldn't thinking about your problems help you find solutions? The truth is, overanalyzing and ruminating on negative events or situations can lead to analysis paralysis, preventing you from ever taking any action at all to address your problems. Habitual negative thinkers tend to be close-minded as well, impeding their ability to think outside the box and see creative solutions. They also might be less likely to reach out to others for help or advice.

Finally, negativity begets more negativity. Remember the feedback loop mentioned earlier? You might have noticed how on days when you wake up on the wrong side of the bed, everything else seems to go wrong, too. You spill coffee on your favorite shirt. You stub your toe. You miss your bus and end up being late for work. Some people believe that you attract negative events and situations by putting out negative energy. However, it could just be that when you are focusing on the negative, that is what you will see. What we place our attention on grows. If you constantly fixate on what is going wrong in your life, you will be more likely to notice every little bad thing and less likely to notice the good things.

How Can I Silence Those Negative Thoughts?

In later chapters, we'll discuss specific strategies and practices to help you tame that negative voice in your head. For now, though, simply focus on becoming aware of your negative thoughts. Take some time to examine what forms they typically take. Understanding the causes of your negative thinking can be an important first step in breaking the habit. We cannot change what we're not aware of.

For example, when you determine what type of negative thinker you are—worst case scenario thinker, blamer, all-or-nothing thinker—you'll begin to notice those thoughts more often as they crop up, providing the opportunity to consciously let them go. Similarly, if you realize you tend to think more negatively in certain situations (at work, with your spouse, etc.), you can begin to think of ways to shift those situations so that you can feel more positive about them. The more you understand your negative thinking patterns, the better prepared you will be to choose the right strategies and practices to help you change them.

You may want to keep a journal or take notes on your smartphone for a few days to help you track your thinking patterns. When you notice yourself caught in a negativity loop, take a moment to jot down some of the details about it. Where were you when the negative thoughts popped up? Who were you with and what were you doing? What form did your negative thoughts take? Were you focused on the past or the future? Did the negativity center on yourself or on external factors (other people, world events, etc.)? How do the negative thoughts make you feel emotionally and physically? Do you notice any tension, tightness, or clenching in your body?

Becoming more aware of your negative thoughts can be uncomfortable. For example, you may begin to see clearly how your negativity has hurt those around you. It can be unpleasant to realize that your behavior has been harmful but such a realization is the only way to make amends and move forward with new behaviors. Awareness is a necessary first step. Your habit of negative thinking did not develop overnight, so breaking the habit will not happen immediately either. In order to truly break the pattern and clear mental space for new habits, you need to be willing to examine your thoughts and work through any uncomfortable emotions or knowledge they may bring up.

Think of your negative thought pattern as a physical illness. In order to know how best to treat you, your doctor would first need to perform tests to determine what type of illness you had and where it stemmed from. Having a clear understanding of the causes and effects of your negative thinking (the source of the infection and the symptoms) will set you up to "treat" it more effectively using the tips and strategies found in the following chapters.

Chapter 2: Why Do I Worry So Much?

If you feel like you spend all of your time worrying over one thing or another, you are far from alone. Worrying is one of the most pervasive forms of negative thinking. We live in an age of instant information and constant communication, and while that brings with it a plethora of benefits, it can also make us very aware of just how much can go wrong in the world. From our health to the economy, from the state of our relationships to social injustice and climate change, we can find enough worries to occupy every waking second if we let ourselves.

In this chapter, we'll take a look at the anatomy of worry and learn some basic practices to help calm your mind and be less fearful as you go through your day-to-day life.

Harmful vs. Normal Worry

A certain amount of worry is normal. Everyone experiences worried thoughts in stressful situations, such as when you're waiting on test results from your doctor or when a dip in the stock market hurts your retirement savings. Expecting to stop worrying altogether is unrealistic; if you put that kind of pressure on yourself, it could lead to even more negative thoughts and lower life satisfaction because you'll feel like you've "failed". Accepting that worrying is normal will help to take some of its power away.

Worrying can even be beneficial to your life in some cases, if it doesn't go to extremes. If you try to avoid worry by sticking your head in the sand and ignoring potentially dangerous or otherwise harmful situations, you won't be able to take steps to prevent them. For example, say your hours at work are being cut, which means your weekly take-home pay will be reduced. If you choose to ignore your worries about your new financial situation, you might not change your spending habits; you could end up going into debt or dipping into your savings unnecessarily. By allowing yourself to feel these realistic worries, however, you will be able to take steps to prevent financial duress. You might look into picking up part-time work or cutting back on more frivolous expenses. In this case, worry can help you react to a situation appropriately.

People who experience a normal amount of worry might also take better care of their health. Some studies have found that when people are worried about potential health problems, such as cancer, they might take better preventive measures, such as getting regular health screenings (Blaszczak-Boxe, 2017). Worry can help us look at life realistically rather than through rose-colored glasses. It allows us to be aware of potential dangers and ultimately navigate life more successfully. In other words, worrying is not necessarily negative in and of itself.

So, when does worrying cross over into problematic negative thinking? If you find that a specific concern is playing on repeat in your head for days or even months at a time, even though there is little evidence that it's something you actually need to worry about, that's a sign that your worrying has reached excessive, unhealthy levels. For example, worrying about your toddler falling down the stairs and deciding to install baby gates is realistic; worrying about media reports of mosquito-borne viruses in the next state over to the point of no longer letting your children play outside is excessive. Acknowledging realistic worries and then taking steps to resolve them is very different than replaying every potential negative outcome over and over again.

Similarly, if you are having difficulty making a decision about how to address or solve a problem in your life, your worrying might be standing in your way. Excessive worrying creates stress and strain in the body, and the natural human response to stress and perceived danger is the Flight, Fight, or Freeze reaction (Fight-Flight-Freeze, n.d.). Freezing up in the face of a decision is a sign that your worrying has reached excessive levels and is causing an unhealthy amount of stress.

Constant, excessive worrying also impacts your mental, emotional, and physical health. If you are having trouble falling or staying asleep because of repetitive worried thoughts or if you are sleeping more than normal in an attempt to escape from your stress, these are signs that your worrying has crossed over into a negative, harmful pattern. Worrying too much can also impact your cognitive function, making it hard for you to concentrate or remember details. If you find yourself feeling more irritable than usual or experiencing frequent headaches, jaw pain, or nausea and abdominal pain, these are all symptoms of excessive worrying. It's important to listen to your body's clues so that you can take steps to reduce your worrying, as long-term stress can lead to more serious health effects, including high blood pressure and ulcers. When you reach this point, worrying itself becomes the enemy that needs to be faced, rather than whatever problem you have been focused on.

In the next section, we'll discuss several ways to help you stop your worries from getting out of control.

How Can I Stop Worrying?

The Cycle of Worry

If left unchecked, your worries will feed on themselves and only grow stronger with time. For example, say you have a large deadline at work that is coming up very quickly. If you are overly worried about meeting this deadline, you might find yourself unable to concentrate on the work itself. Thoughts like, "I'll never get this done. Why didn't I start sooner? There isn't enough time in the day" begin racing through your head, distracting you and causing your worry to gain momentum like a runaway train. The more time and energy you spend worrying about not meeting your deadline, the further away from meeting it you actually get. This is the cycle of worry.

Take another example: your health. Perhaps you are concerned about some physical symptoms you've been experiencing. Instead of motivating you to go see a doctor, your worry might drive you instead to avoid getting medical attention so as not to receive bad news. While in the short term, it might make you feel better to not receive the frightening diagnosis you fear, in the long term, your concerns will just grow as your symptoms persist. In fact, you could end up facing an even worse diagnosis because you did not get help soon enough. In this case, your worry led to avoidance which in the end just gives you more to worry about.

One of the drivers of this cycle of worry is the amygdalae, two small, almond-shaped sections of our brain's temporal lobe. These areas of the brain are responsible for a range of survival instincts, including hunger, sex drive, and the fight-flight-freeze response mentioned earlier. When our bodies are under chronic stress, such as that produced by excessive worrying, it can send our amygdalae into overdrive. This results in heightened feelings of fear, anxiety, and worry. In addition, chronic stress reduces the ability of other regions of our brain, namely the hippocampus and medial prefrontal cortex, to rein in the emotional responses caused by overstimulation of our amygdalae (Ressler, 2010). If our amygdalae have become overactive due to stress and worrying, we can overestimate the actual level of risk or danger faced in a given situation. We will find even more to fear and worry about, thus creating further stress and further overstimulation of this area of the brain.

Question Your Worries

It can be difficult to stop the runaway train of your worries, particularly if worrying is a lifelong habit. As discussed in Chapter 1, the first step in stopping a negative thought pattern like excessive worrying is awareness. Once you have realized that you are worrying too much, you can adopt some simple strategies to help combat the habit.

One simple way to begin to slow down your racing thoughts is to question them. Next time you find yourself carried away by worry, simply take a few deep breaths and ask yourself the following set of questions:

- Is this worry rational or am I engaging in worst case scenario thinking?
- Is this worry something I can solve?

Questioning your worries helps in two ways. First, it acts like the emergency brake in that runaway train of thought, helping to stop it in its tracks. When you worry excessively, you have the same thread of thoughts, and sometimes even the exact same words or images, running through your head over and over again. By introducing a new thought like one of the above questions, you interrupt that repetitive stream. This helps to take away some of the worry's power because it is no longer dominating your mind. The simple act of ceasing to go down the rabbit hole of worry will likely give you immediate emotional relief.

Second, questioning your worries helps you to take action. When we are worried about an event or situation, we often feel helpless, like we are victims at the mercy of fate. Taking action, however small, can help us feel more in control and reduce our fearfulness. If we determine that our worry is rational, we can then decide how to proceed with addressing it. If it is irrational, however, we can choose to let it go; we can do this by using our intellect to point out the flaws in our own thinking and remind ourselves that there is in fact no reason for concern. Similarly, if we determine that our worry is solvable, we can then switch our focus to coming up with ways to solve it. If it is not solvable, we can choose to accept that reality rather than causing ourselves unnecessary stress about something we have no control over. We could instead choose to brainstorm ways to better deal with the uncertainty instead of just ruminating over the problem itself.

Let's take an example. Say you have a new boss who doesn't seem particularly friendly and who has been critical of your work in your last couple of meetings. You find yourself worrying constantly about whether or not your boss likes you; instead of simply doing the best job you can, you're consumed all day with trying to impress him and appear perfect. Your productivity and confidence start to go downhill. Soon you're walking into the office every day anticipating being fired and lying awake at night imagining losing your source of income and being evicted from your home.

We've all let such fear-based thinking run away with us on occasion. You can use the "question your worry" technique to break these fears down and examine them more closely. First, is your worry about your boss not liking you rational? Perhaps it is, but perhaps your new boss is just not overly friendly or demonstrative. More to the point, does it matter whether your boss likes you on a personal level? Plenty of colleagues work together successfully without necessarily having warm personal feelings for one another. What about your worry about getting fired? While your boss has given your work a series of critiques, that is also part of his job. It may not necessarily mean that he is unhappy with your work overall. What about your midnight worries over losing your source of income and ending up homeless? While tragedies do happen, this is clearly the worst case scenario and probably not particularly likely; you can write that particular realm of thought off as fairly irrational and not worthy of your attention at this point.

Now move on to the next question. Of the two fears you identified as at least somewhat rational—that your boss doesn't like you and that he's unhappy with your work and getting ready to fire you—are either of them solvable? If your boss truly does not like you, there is not much you can do about that other than continue to be friendly and professional and hope that he changes his mind with time. We cannot control other people's feelings, so trying too hard to solve this particular worry would be a waste of your energy. What about your worry that he is unhappy with your work? Now this is a problem you can take steps to solve. Make an effort to refocus at work and regain your lost productivity. Be sure to integrate the critiques he's given you into your projects. Perhaps set up a one-on-one meeting with him to discuss his expectations for you and to come up with a list of priorities for you to work on. All of these actions will not only likely make your boss more satisfied with your performance, they'll also make you feel more in control of the situation and less fearful.

The "question your worries" technique can help you see your worried thoughts with more clarity and more objectivity. You can go through this technique in your head or for even more powerful results, write it out in a journal or notebook. That way you can return to it when you feel those old worries beginning to pop up again.

Remember Past Successes

If disappointments have been flooding your mind, then it's only fair you remember past successes, however big or small they are.

When we're lost in constant worrying, it can be hard to believe that what we're fearing won't come to pass or that things will ever work out in our favor. It's easy to get sucked into all-or-nothing thinking at this point and tell ourselves that we'll never be able to accomplish a goal. A simple trick to cutting through these all-or-nothing worries is to bring to mind instances when you succeeded at something or when a situation did go your way. For example, if you're worried about a presentation at work or a test at school, recall a time when you aced a test or gave a perfect sales pitch. This will help to stop the cycle of worry by proving that things do indeed sometimes go well for you and that you have proven yourself to be perfectly capable of accomplishing goals. Recalling your past successes will also give you a much-needed self-esteem boost!

Put Worry on Your Schedule

According to a 2011 study, you might be able to reduce your worrying overall by setting aside specific windows of time in which you allow yourself to worry freely (Brownstein, 2011). Participants in the study were instructed to schedule 30 minutes a day during which they could think about their problems and brainstorm solutions; for the rest of the day, they were instructed to consciously avoid focusing on their worries as much as possible. The idea behind the study is that while telling people to stop worrying altogether is unrealistic, asking people to simply postpone their worrying until a more opportune time can be an effective way to break a pattern of constant worry. Participants who set aside "worry time" experienced reduced stress and higher rates of success in treatment for anxiety disorders and other mental health issues (Brownstein, 2011). Putting worry on your schedule could ultimately help you worry less over time.

Reach Out for Help

Sometimes it can be hard to see our worries clearly. Our own fears loom large in our minds and often seem 100 percent justified to us. Getting an outside perspective can help us to see whether our worries truly are rational and solvable or whether we are giving in to worst case scenario or all-or-nothing thinking. You can reach out to a trusted friend or family member to talk through your concerns. If you feel none of your loved ones are objective enough to help, there are various online and in-person support groups, as well as professionals like counselors, life coaches, and psychiatrists. Any one of these resources may be able to give you a fresh perspective on your worries.

Reaching out to other people can also open your eyes to potential solutions you may not have considered yourself. When we have run through a problem many times in our head, we can often have trouble thinking outside the box and coming up with new ideas. If you are dealing with a rational, solvable worry, a bit of crowd-sourcing might be just what you need to find the right solution.

Don't be afraid to reach out to people. It is good to know that you can rely on someone in your life.

Practice, Practice, Practice

Once again, your habit of excessive worrying did not develop overnight so fixing it will not be an overnight process either. It will take time to fully let go of a worry, particularly if it's one you've held for a long time. Do not beat yourself up when you find yourself getting caught up in worried thoughts. Simply return to the practices above without judgment and try again. With practice, your worries will gradually begin to loosen their grip on your mind and you'll experience longer and longer periods when you're not focusing on your problems.

As you go through this process, remember to celebrate your small successes as well. Any moment in which you can consciously choose to let go of a worry without following it down the rabbit hole is a step in the right direction. Take the time to pause and acknowledge your progress. If you feel comfortable with it, share your achievements with your loved ones or a therapist; their excitement for your success will give you even more motivation to keep going!

Chapter 3: Why Am I So Hard on Myself?

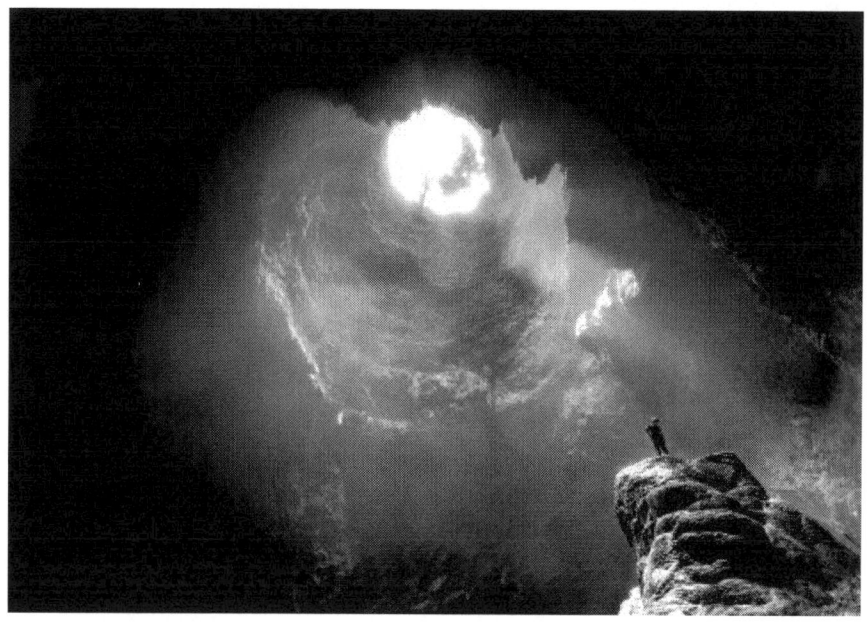

Where Does Negative Self-Talk Come From?

Many of us are our own harshest critics so it should come as no surprise that negative self-talk is another incredibly common form of negative thinking. Negative self-talk can take several forms, including comparing, worst case scenario thinking, all-or-nothing thinking, and overall pessimism about your abilities and prospects. Rather than motivating us to do our best and live up to our potential, this inner critic sets us up for constant failure by creating unrealistic expectations and then berating us when we don't meet them.

Negative self-talk patterns can develop in several ways. You might notice that the harsh voice in your head sounds like someone from your past: a parent, teacher, or former lover, for example. When someone plays an important role in our life, we often take what they say to heart. If an important figure in your life was overly critical of you or demanded perfection, you may have internalized those expectations and beliefs about yourself into your own inner voice. This is particularly true of figures from your childhood, such as parents or other caretakers. For example, if your mother constantly compared you negatively to your older siblings, you might end up telling yourself that you'll never be as successful as your brother. Similarly, if you were raised in a particularly strict religious community or attended a particularly strict or rigorous school, you may have higher expectations for your behavior and abilities and be harder on yourself when you fail to meet them.

We can also pick up negative self-talk patterns from society at large. In the image-obsessed age of social media, it's very easy to compare ourselves to others and find ourselves lacking. For many people, particularly women, this comparison takes the form of poor body image. We are constantly being barraged with images of fit, svelte people with perfect hair and impeccable clothing. Even if we know on a rational level that these images are not realistic, our subconscious mind still soaks them in as the expected standard. When we quite understandably are not able to live up to these standards, we can experience low self-esteem, feelings of sadness, hopelessness, or failure. This negative thinking can have health effects as well; we may stop engaging in healthy behaviors, thinking, "Well, what's the point of trying to eat healthy and exercise? I'll never look like that anyway." People with low self-esteem and poor body image can also develop serious eating disorders like anorexia nervosa or bulimia; this is particularly common among adolescents. A 2013 study found that young teenagers who compared themselves with television characters of the same sex had a higher likelihood of being dissatisfied with their own physical looks. The female participants of the study showed higher rates of dissatisfaction with their weight and those with poor body image were more likely to have engaged in some type of diet in the previous year (Vitelli, 2013).

Society can also put unrealistic expectations on us in terms of wealth, career, education, or family. Just as with body image, these expectations can lead us to engage in negative self-talk. For example, if we grew up in a community or family in which getting married and having children is highly praised, we might feel a sense of failure if we do not find the right partner until later in life or if we are unable to have children.

How Can I Stop Negative Self-Talk?

Just like any other form of negative thinking, it is normal to fall prey to self-judgment and negative self-talk from time to time. We will naturally feel sad, disappointed, or even ashamed when we fail to achieve a goal or when we feel that we have not lived up to our values or have let down a loved one. When your self-image is made up entirely of negative thoughts about yourself, though, it is time to tackle the problem. Constant negative self-talk can lower your self-esteem, hurt your relationships, create social isolation, lower your productivity and financial prospects, limit your creativity and joy, and even lead to more serious mental health issues.

Here are a few simple strategies to get you started on creating a healthier, more positive self-image.

Question Your Thoughts

Just like when we tackled constant worry in the last chapter, questioning our negative self-talk is an excellent way to begin dismantling the habit. As the common saying goes, don't believe everything you think. There are a few basic questions you can use to examine the validity of your negative self-talk.

- **Whose voice is this?** When you find yourself caught up in self-criticism, take a moment to stop and really listen to the words and tone you are using. Does it sound like you or does it sound like someone from your past? If you have unconsciously taken on expectations, judgments, or criticisms from loved ones or authority figures, now is the time to begin letting them go. You are not obligated to carry other people's expectations. Your life is your own and you can determine for yourself what standards you believe in and choose to live by. If you identify a certain pattern of thinking as the voice of someone else, come up with a response to use whenever that thought crops up. For example, perhaps you constantly tell yourself that you're a failure for not going to college and you have determined that this line of thinking ("Only losers don't go to college") stems from a former teacher. You could respond with, "I have my own definition of success. I can and will continue to accomplish great things."

- **Is there evidence to back up this thought?** Just like we paused to examine whether our worries were rational, we can examine whether our self-criticisms are valid. We tend to believe what we tell ourselves, particularly what we say repetitively, but oftentimes our negative thinking is an exaggeration of reality. When you take the time to actually challenge your thoughts and ask, "Is this true?" you will likely find that it is not, at least not entirely. For example, maybe you constantly question your relationships and think, "They're probably only friends with me out of pity." If you challenge this thought, you'll likely see that it is a skewed perspective and that there have been plenty of instances in your life in which you experienced deep, authentic friendships with people who love you.

- **Is this thought kind? Would I say this to a friend?** Once you take the time to become aware of your self-talk, you might be surprised by just how mean you are to yourself. We tend to say things about ourselves that we would never say about a friend, family member, or even a stranger. You deserve just as much respect and kindness as anyone else in the world, both from others and from yourself. Next time you start beating yourself up for gaining a few pounds or for making a mistake at work, stop and ask yourself, "Would I say this to a friend?" If the answer is no, then stop.

Change What You Can

Sometimes in the course of your negative self-talk, you will hit on a problem that is actually at least partially valid. For example, you might beat yourself up for being lazy and not following through with things. After using the above questions, you might in fact determine that this criticism has some validity to it: you rarely follow through on your stated goals. In this instance, your negative self-talk can be used to make positive life changes. You can resolve to change your ways and begin setting small, attainable goals to improve your follow-through.

You'll not only stop a bad habit, you'll also increase your self-esteem by proving to yourself that you are capable and disciplined. It's important, however, to not get further carried away by your original negative thought. If you determine that you do in fact have problems following through with things, it could be very easy to slip deeper into self-criticism and even self-loathing. Rather than beat yourself up for having uncovered a valid self-criticism, use it as motivation to forgive yourself and move forward with a new way of living.

Release Judgment of Your Thoughts

We touched on this a bit in the previous point, but one of the most crucial steps in reducing your negative self-talk is to release your judgment of your thoughts. If you have engaged in negative self-talk for most of your life, attempting to stop that habit might in itself bring up new negative self-talk patterns. You might begin to beat yourself up for being so negative!

To prevent this, focus on releasing your negative thoughts in a forgiving, non-judgmental way. You can create statements or mantras to help with this process. Using the previous example of a lack of follow-through, you could repeat to yourself or write in your journal, "I forgive myself for not following through with things in the past." If you're feeling overwhelmed by your negative thinking itself, you could use a statement like, "It's okay to be angry with myself for developing this habit." This releases the judgment surrounding your emotions, making it easier to process them and then move on from them effectively.

Use Positive Affirmations

While not everyone finds positive affirmations helpful, many people have used them with great success to shift their mindset and change negative thought patterns. Positive affirmations are motivational or inspiring statements that you repeat to yourself in order to change a habit. Once you have identified negative self-talk patterns that you want to stop, you can create positive affirmations to inspire change. Repeat these affirmations multiple times throughout the day; you can set reminders on your phone, post them on your bathroom mirror, or write them out ten times in your journal before bed. The more you repeat them, the deeper they will settle into your mind and become your new habit of thinking.

Let's say you struggle with negative self-talk surrounding your body image. Rather than focusing on affirmations about what you're directly unhappy with, such as your weight, focus on the broader idea of your body and health. You could create statements like, "I honor my body with healthy amounts of food and exercise", "I deserve to feel good in my body", or "My body is the vessel for my soul". These types of affirmations take the focus off your pain point—in this case, your weight—and help you gain a more expansive perspective.

When you first start using positive affirmations, they might feel fake or forced. This is perfectly natural. You likely didn't believe it fully the first time someone told you that you were stupid or incapable; those beliefs only became integrated into your self-image over time and with repetition. Positive beliefs work the same way. You may not believe them right away but it is important to stick with the practice. With time and repetition, you will find your thinking naturally drawn toward more positive channels.

List Your Positive Qualities

Take some time to list in writing all of your positive traits and qualities. You can do this weekly or even daily at first to build your mental positivity muscle. This is another exercise in which you might have to "fake it 'til you make it." It likely won't feel natural at first to compliment yourself if you've been used to doing the opposite. You may even feel like you're lying or making things up. In the beginning, don't try to force yourself to find something positive to say about aspects of your life that generally draw on your self-criticism. For example, if your negative self-talk tends to center on your body image, don't make yourself think of positive things to say about your body, at least not until you've done the practice regularly for a while. Instead, focus on areas of your life outside of your body that you are happy with or proud of. You could list your intelligence, your friendliness, your punctuality—anything that pleases you about yourself.

Once you have been working on your positivity list for a while, then you can turn to the areas of real struggle for you. You might begin to write down things that your body has allowed you to do, such as have children or take your dog for hikes. You might focus on certain aspects of your physical appearance that you do like; while you might not be happy with your weight, you might love your eyes, the color of your hair, or your smile. Regularly putting down in writing the things you like and respect about yourself is a powerful way to break through the cloud of self-judgment you may have been living under.

Ask for Help

Like in our chapter on worry, asking for help to identify and dismantle your negative self-talk patterns can be incredibly useful. Other people will be able to tell you when you are being unreasonably hard on yourself. They will also be able to help balance your negative self-talk by highlighting your strengths and positive attributes; you can even ask for a loved one's help with your positivity list. Other people can also make sure you are addressing your problems in a safe way. If your negative self-talk stems from more serious issues like childhood abuse or trauma, it is imperative to seek the help of a professional like a counselor or psychiatrist in order to help you process and heal from those past experiences.

Do not keep your emotions bottled up. It is not going to help you in any way. Some people might think that they don't want to impose on others. While others might refuse to talk about what is bothering them out of politeness. But not speaking about your problems and simply being silent while they cause you much mental anguish and distress is only going to cause you harm. By keeping them inside, you are allowing them to fester and worsen. You might be able to avoid talking about them for a while or distract yourself long enough to stay far from their effects, but eventually they catch up to you and when they do, you are usually not prepared for them. You might also start feeling the effects of depression and other mental health problems.

If you feel uncomfortable talking about your problems completely to someone, then try talking about them in parts. Take a small part of the problem and discuss it with your friends and family. Then you can think about talking to them further when you feel comfortable. I have talked about this in the next chapter, where you will find out how to communicate problems with people effectively.

Additionally, do not think that seeking help makes you appear weak. On the contrary, seeking help shows strength in character. You are letting people know that you are not going to let your problems define you. You are going to face them head-on. And here is the truth; nobody said you have to face your problems alone. If you can get some help, great! Make the most out of it.

The past two chapters have focused on ways to address two common and specific types of negative thinking: worry and comparison/negative self-talk. In the next chapter, we turn our attention more broadly to how to control and reduce overthinking and negative thinking in general. We begin with the basics: how to regain control of your thoughts.

Chapter 4: How Can I Control My Thoughts?

Picture a snowball rolling down a mountain. It starts out small but as time goes on, the snowball picks up speed, gains momentum, and grows in size. Soon that little snowball is barreling out of control, wiping out anything in its path.

Your habit of negative thinking works in much the same way. It might begin with just a random thought here and there. "I hate Mondays." "Why do I always get stuck behind the slowest driver?" "Ugh, my husband left dirty dishes in the sink again." These tiny thoughts can creep into your mind without you even really noticing them, but over time, they grow in size and power. They begin to dominate your mental chatter, your conversations, and even your dreams. Eventually they take over your entire mental process, distorting your perspective of reality, the world around you, other people, and even yourself.

The average person has between 12,000 and 60,000 thoughts per day; out of those thousands of thoughts, an estimated 80 percent are negative and 95 percent are repetitive (Hardy, 2018). You likely would not choose to listen to the same sad song all day every day or watch the same sad movie every night. You wouldn't do these things because you know that in the end, they will not make you feel good! When you do not address your negative thinking, though, you are essentially choosing to do exactly the same thing. You are choosing to surround yourself with sadness, anger, resentment, frustration, fear, and worry. You likely are not doing it consciously, but you are choosing daily actions that just flat out will not make you feel good.

The good news is that you can choose differently. You can change your mind. Once you become aware that negative thinking has become a problem in your life, you can begin to consciously choose to let it go. If you've engaged in negative thinking for a long time, possibly even your entire life, it probably seems daunting to try to break the habit. But just like you can train your body in the gym to get stronger and faster, you can also train your brain. You can learn to control your mind and rein in your negative thinking, no matter what form it takes. In this chapter, we'll go over some simple practices and strategies to help you develop this control.

The practices outlined here will take time, effort, and dedication to implement in your life, but just as it's important to take care of your body with proper exercise, it's crucial to take care of your mental health as well. Your mind impacts literally every facet of your life so you need to make sure it's in the best shape possible in order to live up to your fullest potential for both success and happiness.

How to Control Your Mind

Become the Conscious Observer of Your Thoughts

On a moment-to-moment basis, our thoughts tend to act like white noise or background music. They flow through our mind effortlessly without attracting much notice. They also do not hang around for too long; if left to their own devices, thoughts pass through our minds quickly. One minute, you're thinking about what to cook for dinner and then suddenly you find yourself reminiscing about something funny your spouse said that morning. Sometimes, though, we become attached to a particular thought and begin to follow it. That one thought leads to another related thought and another and soon you have lost an hour of your time following this train of thought.

Sometimes this habit can be pleasant, like when you get lost in a fun daydream. If you become attached to a negative thought, though, you can quickly get sucked down a rabbit hole of negativity. This is when that one small snowball of a negative thought picks up speed and starts to become an avalanche.

There is no way to stop an avalanche once it has started. The only way to stop an avalanche is to prevent it from occurring in the first place. While it's not completely impossible to stop the spiral of negative thoughts, it's much easier to prevent that spiral from even starting. How do you do this?

Awareness

As we said before, you cannot change what you are not aware of. In order to stop following the path of random negative thoughts, in order to learn how to just let them pop into your mind and then pop back out again naturally, you first need to see your thoughts. You need to learn to observe your thoughts consciously, neutrally, and non-judgmentally.

Whenever you are presented with a situation, try and notice the way you react to it. Were you angry when the driver cut you off in front of you? Was the reason for your anger the driver or something bigger?

When you begin to evaluate your situation, you might notice that things are not as clear-cut as they seem.

Perform a Brain-Dump

When the garbage in your house begins to fill up, what do you do? You obviously empty the trash can. You don't want that pile spilling over!

Take the time to write down your thoughts to perform a brain dump.

It's the same with your brain. Not all the information you have in your brain might be useful to you. Or you might be feeling down about your personal life or work. Sometimes, it feels as though there is a hurricane going through your brain and you are unable to focus on a thought or add new thoughts to your brain. It might truly become overwhelming for you to think.

But why exactly does your brain become overwhelmed?

Think of your thoughts like the tabs of your internet browser. You have opened a few tabs because you deem them important. As more tasks get added to your life, you open even more tabs. However, you forget to close the old ones. Eventually, you have a hundred tabs open and you are shifting from one tab to another, trying to get a bearing on your thoughts.

In such cases, you perform a brain dump.

A brain dump is a process where you get the thoughts out of your head so that you can deal with them. The process helps you focus on one thought at a time and even prioritize them. So how do you do a brain dump?

Step 1: Get a Pen and Paper (Or You Can Use a Word Processor)

I recommend using a pen and paper because it gets your brain to focus on what you are writing. When your brain is focused, you are able to process information better.

Step 2: Make a List

Your next step is to write down every plan or activity that comes to your mind. Do you have a project you need to finish at work? Perhaps a birthday party that you need to attend? Did you make movie plans with someone? Whatever it is, write it down on a sheet of paper.

Step 3: Take a Walk

When you have finished listing as many things as you can remember, get up from your place and take a walk. Walk for about 5 to 10 minutes and then return to the sheet of paper. Focus on it again and you might remember some things that you hadn't thought of earlier. Add them to the list as well.

At this point, you might have a pretty big list in front of you.

Step 4: Categorize

Start categorizing your list into various sections. Here is an example that you can make use of:

- Personal
- Home
- Work

- Freelancing Stuff
- Projects
- Work Ideas
- Plans
- Errands
- Important Dates

You can create your own list based on your requirements. But make sure that you have a list that ties in with your requirements and goals.

Step 5: Break Down the Projects

Now take each task and break them into smaller objectives. Something as simple as "get a carton of milk on the way home" does not have to be broken down any further. But if you have a task such as "complete your work project by the end of the week," then find ways to break it down into manageable and achievable portions.

This step is not mandatory. So, if you think that you cannot break down any tasks, then don't force it.

Step 6: Add Schedules

In this step, you are going to prioritize your tasks. Look through the list and find out all the tasks that you can complete immediately. Then move on to the next set of tasks in order of priority. As you move down the list, make sure that you are giving a timeframe for those tasks that cannot be completed at a specific time.

Another way that you can split the tasks is by the below categories:

- Tasks that should be done today
- Tasks to complete within this week
- Tasks to complete within this month
- Things to do after this month
- Unimportant things

Anything that you place into the unimportant things category should be forgotten about since they don't matter. You should be critical about your list. Your list should ideally be concise so that you can sort through the important things. The main purpose of a brain dump is to filter out the unwanted ideas that flood your mind.

Step 7: Start Working

As soon as you have completed your list, focus on the task that you have to do immediately. The earlier you can start working, the faster you can get through the tasks.

The list can always increase in length. If you feel that you have more to add, then add them and follow the steps above to give them a timeframe or schedule.

Get Out of Your Head and into Your Body

It is tempting to entertain your thoughts. There is a need to solve them in your head. You brood over them thinking that you are going to find an answer to them only to realize that the only thing you managed to accomplish was a splitting headache.

Don't spend too much time on your thoughts. Rather, write down the problem on a piece of paper. Then use the steps below to deal with it.

Step 1: Identify the Problem

Write down the nature of the problem and other details that you can add to the list. For example, let us say that you are a graphic designer and you have to create 5 creative samples of an advertisement. Note down the problem by using the questions below:

- What do you have to do?
- Are there any specific requests?
- What should you avoid?
- What would you consider as a job well done?
- What do you think shows poor quality?
- Does the client have any objectives that they would like to focus on?

Add other questions that you feel are pertinent to gather more information about the task.

Step 2: Provide Research Materials (If Required)

- Do you have any sources of information that you would like to refer to?
- Can you get any help solving the problem? It could be your friends or your colleagues.

- Do you think you can put in a request to your boss for assistance?
- Do you have samples that you can use to inspire you?

Whatever materials you have that can help you can be added to this section.

Step 3: Provide Solutions

Take your time to come up with as many solutions as you can for the problem. List down any creative ideas that you think can help you finish the tasks quicker. Make sure that you list down the details of the solution. Do not just keep bullet points of what you would like to do. You need to have a written record of what you would like to do in case you forget the solution in the future.

Step 4: Provide Alternatives

Let us assume that the worst comes to pass and you are unable to complete the tasks on time. What do you do then? Do you have an alternative strategy? Can you deal with any delays that might arise during the completion of the task? What would you do if you lost creative inspiration? Make sure that you have a list of all available alternatives to deal with a plethora of unexpected circumstances.

Step 5: Plan of Action

There is no point in making a plan if you have no actions to back it up. Your final step is to list down all the actions that you are going to take in order to complete the task at hand.

Make sure you give schedules and timeframes for the actions. Do not give too much wiggle room to complete the tasks. When you give your mind the chance to look for chances to delay your work or take long breaks, then rest assured, it usually does look for a way to ease things.

Now that you have a plan set for your project, there is another important question you might have to deal with; what happens if you cannot create a plan to deal with your problem or task?

In that case, you have nothing to worry about because events are beyond your control. You should focus on removing the worries you have about the problem out of your head and keep your attention focused on the things that you can handle in front of you. This might be tricky. You might be tempted to return to the problem. But unless you can deal with it, you shouldn't be thinking about it too much.

Become Emotionally Strong

Your mind can sometimes wander when it is faced with an emotional task. Emotions can also distract you from the things that are important, cause unwanted levels of stress, or even project unhealthy negativity into your mind.

While it is not wrong to show your emotional side, it is not right to let your emotions take control of your life too much. Being emotionally strong allows you to approach your life with tact and rational behavior.

But how can one become emotionally strong? Here are some ways to go about it.

Set Boundaries

Whether it is with your friends, family members, relatives, or even your colleagues, it is important that you set some boundaries for yourself. If you do this, you will understand where you stand in all matters of life. People won't take advantage of your kindness or treat your emotions as though they did not matter. They won't just start assuming that they can do anything to you. When you create a degree of tolerance and acceptance, then you are effectively laying down the foundation for emotional strength.

Forget the Past

Do not let the past become a ghost in your life, haunting you at every turn and reminding you of your failures, pain, disappointments, incapabilities, or weaknesses. Do not try to emotionally autopsy your past. Rather, try and learn from them. Figure out how you can use them to become a better person. In fact, the past does not exist. The flow of time cannot go backwards (despite what the science-fiction movies tell you). Your past is officially a thing only present in memories. Let it stay that way. Your only reason for thinking about them is to plan the future.

Ask for Help

Whether you simply need the company of your friends or a shoulder to cry on, reach out to someone. Having people listen to you not only lightens the burden, but also reminds you that you are not alone in this world. If you need help, don't be afraid to ask. Do not automatically label yourself as a burden. Even if people think you are a burden to them, do not think of yourself as such. You should be cutting ties with such people, as they have made their intentions clear. Do not surround yourself with toxic people, who only attach labels on you and are absent whenever you need them the most.

Discover the Joy of Your Company

You are the protagonist of your story. If you have watched the recent Avengers movie, then you might have a favorite character. It could be Iron Man or it could be Black Widow, but there are characters you love because they are cool, smart, confident, powerful, or for any other reason. In the same way, look at the things that make you seem awesome in your eyes. Why do you love you? What makes you special? What do you like to do?

As you discover more about yourself, you will have more reasons to enjoy your own company. Try to engage in your passions or activities that you enjoy doing.

Enjoy spending time by yourself.

Take Care of Your Body

The body is a temple; respect it and take care of it. Don't allow your health to deteriorate. Try and exercise as frequently as possible. Even brisk jogging will do. Eat a well-balanced meal. Make sure that you are keeping your body in peak condition. Avoid using substances such as nicotine, alcohol, and caffeine too much.

And while you are taking care of your body, make sure that you...

...Take Care of Your Mind

The mind is a powerful tool. And just like all tools, it can suffer wear and tear over time. Keep healthy mental habits so that you keep your mind fit. Try and meditate. Engage in mentally stimulating activities. Do not overload your mind and give yourself as much rest as possible.

And if you really have to, then go ahead and take a vacation. You probably deserve it.

Forget Your Drama

In today's world, almost everything is documented on social media. People are tempted to get into discussions and spend their mental energy trying to win over random strangers on the internet. Remember to pick your battles. Do not start an argument with each and every person you meet online. At the same time, do not look to engage in an emotional argument with people in your life if you really don't have to. Does someone prefer something that you do not like? Let it go. Live and let live. Do you feel like people have different opinions on a particular subject? Then don't try too hard to bring them on your side.

Benefits of a Thoughts Journal

One of the ways to deal with overwhelming thoughts or emotions is to express them in healthy ways. Rather than break objects when you are angry or frustrated, you can instead choose to divert all that energy into something more rewarding.

This is where a journal becomes useful. When you use a journal, you:

- Are able to manage anxiety
- Can reduce stress effectively
- Can cope with depression

So how do you record your thoughts in a journal effectively? Here are a few tips that you can use:

Journal Tip #1: Try to Write Every day

Be consistent when you journal your thoughts and ideas. Ideally, you should be journaling your thoughts every day. If you feel that writing in a book is not efficient, then you can make use of the numerous journal software and applications that are available. This way, you don't have to worry about running out of pages. You do not need to spend an hour or so writing. Simply set aside a few minutes and describe your day. Talk about anything that you would like to express. If you feel that you had reacted negatively or experienced negative thoughts or emotions, then mention the reason for the negativity. Allow yourself to express freely. When you are done, go back and read your entry. Think about the situation and see if you can write down a possible solution for the outburst of negative thoughts or reaction. Don't worry if you cannot find a proper solution. You will get the time to deal with your negative emotions, as we will discuss in the next chapter. For now, just focus on keeping your journal entries consistent.

Journal Tip #2: Carry Your Journal with You

Try to keep your pen and paper or your journal application with you at all times. This way, you can create an entry any time you feel like it. Write down the entry when the thoughts are fresh in your memory so that you can express yourself better.

Journal Tip #3: You Don't Have to Be a Writer

The important rule of journal writing is this: write whatever feels right! Don't worry about how you sound. This is your journal and it should be used to express yourself freely. It is your private space to pen your thoughts and discuss the things that matter to you. Do not hold back the words. Sometimes, you might be surprised by the emotions behind your words. Do not be alarmed by it. Let the words flow through your hands freely. And you don't have to worry about what others think. After all, it is not like you are going to publish your journal!

Journal Tip #4: Your Journal, Your Rules

If you feel like you would like to share your journal with someone, but are not sure if it is the right thing to do, then try the following instead. Take a journal entry that you would like to talk about and then discuss that with your friends or family. See if you are comfortable communicating your thoughts to them. Then check if they are receptive to your thoughts and emotions. If you feel comfortable talking to them, then you can choose to share more of your journal entries.

The Power of Sleep

A good night's sleep is something we all crave to a point where we feel like the phrase "good night's sleep" is nothing but a myth.

The reality is that a good night's sleep is as important as a healthy diet and exercise. In fact, if you are working out, then one of the routines that you have to incorporate into your life is a good night's rest.

In today's fast-paced world, people are finding it difficult to get the required hours of sleep. At the same time, the quality of sleep has decreased as well. Let us see why sleep is important.

Weight Gain

Did you ever think that sleep could actually be connected to weight gain? Seems like a farfetched idea, doesn't it? In fact, one might claim that I am creating connections when none exist. Sadly, there does exist a link between poor sleep and weight gain, which has also been documented by a research (Cappuccio et al., 2008). Based on the results of the study, children and adults who do not get the recommended sleep hours are 55% to 85% more likely to become obese.

Good Sleep = Fewer Calories

When you get a good night's sleep, then your mind is active. It only requires the necessary amount of nutrition that you feed it on a daily basis. However, when you are sleep deprived, the body and mind require even more energy to function normally. Eventually, people start consuming more coffee and more sugar, just to get through the day. The body also increases the production of ghrelin, which is the hormone that triggers appetite in the body.

Concentration and Productivity

When you get a good night's sleep, then your body arranges the memories, thoughts, and ideas of the previous day. It does this so that when you wake up in the morning, it is as though your mind has a clean slate to start with. You are able to absorb memories better, which increases the brain's concentration levels, and eventually contributes to better productivity.

What happens if you are sleep deprived? Firstly, all those memories from the previous day won't be arranged and catalogued properly by your brain. You wake up with your head full of thoughts, which cause headaches in some people. Secondly, the brain cannot store more memories. It is like adding water to a cup that is already full. Your concentration then begins to diminish and you find yourself unable to store more information. When you can't take in new information, then you won't be able to take in the information that matters. For example, let's say that you have to manage an important business event for your company. You are in charge of everything, from finances to the logistics to marketing of the event. Since your brain is unable to take in more information, you begin to forget things easily. You might have taken into account a piece of information recently, but because of your memory, you won't be able to recollect it because your brain disperses the information. Your productivity lowers and that eventually starts showing in your work.

Getting Physical

Sleep also increases physical performance. With proper sleep, you feel well-rested. It's like putting the battery of your mobile device to charge; after you disconnect the charger, you are going to have longer-lasting battery power. In fact, research conducted on poor sleep has shown that proper sleep has improved performances in basketball players (Mah, C. D., Mah, K. E., Kezirian, & Dement, 2011).

Glucose

Lack of sleep affects blood sugar levels and also decreases insulin sensitivity. As you might know, insulin is a hormone produced by the body that creates glucose from carbohydrates from the food that you consume. The hormone keeps your blood sugar levels from becoming too high, a condition called hyperglycemia, or too low, known as hypoglycemia. When the sensitivity of insulin reduces, then it won't be able to detect the carbohydrates in the body. This might prevent it from getting the required amount of glucose into the body, which eventually leads to hypoglycemia.

Depression

The links between sleep and mental state is a complicated one. When you have improper sleep patterns, then your brain loses its mental strength. This brings about big shifts in your emotions. These emotional fluctuations are exhausting for the brain to deal with. Imagine this scenario playing out. You have spent a long day at work and you are exhausted beyond belief. All you can think of is just relaxing for a bit. However, you realize that you still have so many chores to take care of. You would not exactly be at your peak performance now, would you? Your brain goes through the same process. It is too exhausted to deal with the emotional fluctuations and just lets your mind feel the full brunt of all emotions it receives, good or bad. When all the negative emotions you feel are unfiltered, you officially have a recipe for poor mental health. All of the negative emotions eventually cause depression, stress, and even anxiety.

How to Get Proper Sleep?

There are a few tricks you can use to improve the quality of your sleep.

Increase Daylight Exposure

Your body has a natural method of keeping time known as the circadian rhythm. This rhythm is based on the different times of the day. It tells your hormones, body, and brain when to stay awake and when it is time to rest. Exposure to natural sunlight helps you maintain your circadian rhythm. Have you ever been in a situation where you have been spending so much time indoors that when you look outside the window or step outside, you are surprised that so much time has passed and it is already dark? If you find yourself in such situations, then you need to change your habits. Continually disrupting your circadian rhythm causes your body to keep you awake, thinking that it is not time for bed. Eventually, it is pushing past the limits of exhaustion and you are not aware of it. This causes insomnia and you end up feeling sleepy way later than you should, causing you to receive less sleep.

Get yourself some natural sunlight. Try and take breaks outside as much as possible in order to get your body used to the time of day.

Blue Light Exposure

Daylight improves sleep patterns. But what about lights at night?

Research has shown that nighttime light exposure, especially blue light, causes you to lose sleep (Fonken et al., 2010). Once again, this has got to do with your circadian rhythm. The blue light confuses the brain into thinking that it is still daytime. Your brain becomes instantly more alert. This is why many people stay on their mobile devices, going through their social media feed until late into the night. They claim that they use their phones because they are unable to sleep, little do they know that they are unable to sleep *because* they are using their phones. When people who are used to scrolling through their mobile devices late at night try to sleep early, it becomes a bit of a challenge for them.

Avoid Caffeine Late at Night

Caffeine increases focus and energy. Which is why having it late at night only makes you want to stay up late. The caffeine enters your nervous system and stimulates it, preventing your body from relaxing late at night.

Avoid Irregular Sleep Patterns

Your body will give you a signal to fall asleep at certain times of the day because it is used to the fact that you fall asleep at the same time every day. In fact, have you ever experienced a time where you automatically wake up in the morning without the help of your alarm? You often wonder if you are getting used to waking up at that particular time. The truth is; you are. When you stick to a schedule, the body automatically adjusts its internal clock to support your timings. But what happens when you keep disrupting this schedule? Well, in that case, your body simply starts giving you mixed signals. You start feeling tired when you are not supposed to, such as in the middle of your work.

Don't Consume Too Much Alcohol

Better yet, avoid alcohol altogether. Alcohol is known to increase the causes of sleep apnea (Issa & Sullivan, 1982).

Sleep apnea is a serious sleep disorder that is characterized by irregular breathing during sleep. As you drift off to sleep, your breathing stops and starts up again without any warning.

Because of this breathing pattern, you might not get a good night's sleep. This causes you to have poor sleep. When you wake up in the morning, you are left feeling drowsy and tired. Sleep apnea is even dangerous as you might wake up gasping for air. In other words, you are at a risk of suffocating while you sleep, which is a definitely frightening prospect.

Improve Bedroom Conditions

Is your bedroom too hot? Do you have too much light filtering through the curtains? Do you smell something odd or hear the sounds of dripping water from the kitchen? All of these sounds, sights, and smells distract your brain from focusing on sleep. Certain people are used to disturbances and have trained their brain to ignore them during sleep. But that only accounts for a small part of the population. Most people are not used to facing disturbances during sleep.

Your bedroom should be a place where you can relax. Try and optimize your bedroom settings. Remove any artificial light from electronic devices such as digital clocks, computers, and mobile devices. Make sure that your bedroom is a quiet and relaxed place for you to get a good night's sleep.

Clear Your Mind in the Evening

Try not to go to bed with your head filled with thoughts. If you want to, you can meditate for a while before you head to bed. You can also listen to relaxing music, take a warm bath, or read a book to encourage you to fall asleep. One particular method may not work for you so try experimenting until you find the best way to put yourself to sleep.

Check Up

You might not have any sleep disorders, but it is better to get expert advice on the matter. Head to your local doctor and see if you need to receive treatment for any sleep conditions. No one likes to be told that they have a sleep disorder. However, it is far better to know that there is something and get it treated than ignore it until it becomes worse.

Make Sure You Have a Comfortable Bed

Some people wonder why it is that they find it more comfortable to sleep in a hotel.

The reason is simple. Hotel beds are made for comfort. Make sure that you bring the same level of comfort to your bed as well. If you need two pillows, add them. Need a thick blanket? Get one. With proper sleeping conditions, you will avoid problems such as backaches, neck stiffness, numbness in various parts of the body, and other physical problems.

Exercise and Yoga

But not before bed! You do not want to pump your body full of adrenaline right before you catch some Zs. When you exercise, you are encouraging your body to get rid of all your muscle tension, relaxing them. The same goes for yoga as well. When you eventually fall asleep, your body is ready to relax.

Avoid Fluids

Do not drink too much fluid before going to bed. This causes nocturia, which is a condition where you feel compelled to urinate excessively during the night. This causes you to repeatedly wake up in the middle of the night, interrupting a good night's sleep. In some cases, people find it difficult to head back to sleep once they are woken up by nocturia.

Avoid drinking fluids at least 1 or 2 hours before you head to bed.

Bottom Line

If you find yourself getting less sleep than required, then try and evaluate your sleep patterns, conditions, and your health. Check and see if the environment you are sleeping in is comfortable. If your sleeping patterns are irregular, then you can work on that. Check that you are eating a proper diet before heading to bed (try not to eat too close to bedtime) and that you are getting proper exercises during the day. Look through the solutions provided above and then see if any applies to your situation. And if you feel that you have tried everything and you still have difficulty sleeping, don't hesitate to visit the doctor. It's better to receive a proper solution to your problem.

Chapter 5: How Can I Start Thinking Positively?

Believe in yourself!

Have faith in what you do!

Once cannot be happy with that they do without a reasonable amount of confidence in themselves. "Believe in yourself" might sound like a cliché statement at this point, having heard it numerous times in movies, social platforms, or verbally from people close to you. It might have lost its 'charm' after having been repeated over and over again.

But there is a truth to the statement.

A woman was once broke and living in poverty. On a train from Manchester to London, she wrote a book about a magical place filled with dragons, witches, and strange objects.

The woman was J. K. Rowling, who went on to write one of the most influential book series in fiction; Harry Potter.

A man was fired from the company that he created. He went on to build his own company, grew it, and bought the original company.

The man was Steve Jobs and the company he acquired was Apple.

A man lived in poverty stricken situations with his young son. But that did not stop him from becoming a millionaire through an investment firm that he created.

The man was Chris Gardner and he was also the focus of Will Smith's character in the movie The Pursuit of Happyness.

All of these people were at a low point in their lives. Some of them were going through mental health issues, such as J.K. Rowling, while others had lost the very thing that they put their effort into building, as in the case of Steve Jobs. At any point after their tragic and disappointing encounters, they could have just thrown their hands in the air and just admitted defeat. They could have let life carry them wherever it could. No one would blame them. After all, how many more defeats could they take?

But that is not what they did. We have 7 Harry Potter books. Apple grew to become the first trillion-dollar company. People still quote dialogue from the movie The Pursuit of Happyness.

All of the above situations are possible because people decided that they would rather get back to doing something than give up with nothing.

Yet, what's the point of doing something if one does not believe in their endeavors? Let me give you an example so that I can explain this point a little better.

Have you ever heard of a state of mind called line hypnosis? If you have watched assembly line workers, then you might realize that they start doing their work in automation. To them, the process remains the same. They simply have to follow a predetermined set of steps to complete their tasks. Once they get used to the task, they start doing it without paying attention to it. Eventually, their mind drifts off to other ideas, memories, and thoughts as they complete their work. That is because they don't require their conscious mind to put in any effort. Their subconscious mind – now well-versed with the steps of the process – takes over their tasks while they can use their conscious mind to think about insipid affairs. When the assembly line workers enter into this dreamlike state, they are said to be experiencing line hypnosis.

The assembly line workers have only one job; they simply have to repeat tasks over and over again, never knowing if they are going to achieve something big or maybe aim for a corner office. To most of them, their workspace is where they belong. That does not mean they are bad at their job. It merely means that they have reached a point where they are not finding anything stimulating in their environment. Now imagine yourself in their position where you are currently experiencing a case of line hypnosis; do you believe in the endeavor you are doing or would you wish for something more? Imagine doing the same thing from one day to the next. What do you believe in that will make you continue doing it?

You see, regardless of whether you choose to stay in the assembly line job or not, you still have to believe in your choice.

If you choose to stay in the assembly line job, then you have to believe that it is benefiting you in some way or helping you reach a goal. If, on the other hand, you have chosen to move on, you have to believe that there is something worth achieving outside the assembly line job. But how is this related to believing in yourself?

If you don't believe in yourself, then you have no motivation to do anything. You complete your tasks because you should, not because you want to. It does not matter if you are in an assembly line job or otherwise, you are going to go through your life with the same level of care and attention. Your entire life is going to feel like an assembly line job; a series of repetitions, uninspiring moments, and minimal successes. Eventually, your life is going to be one big line hypnosis.

"Believe in yourself" is just one of the many positive ideas that you need in your life.

Then again, life is what we are trying to influence with our positive emotions. And there is something that you should know about life itself.

Life Has Two Faces

Imagine a married couple had a newborn son.

One day, the mother walked up to the baby's crib, picked up a baby rattle and shook it. The baby did not react. She thought that it was probably because the baby was coming out of sleep and hadn't gotten used to the sounds of his environment yet. This time, she decided to shake the rattle a little harder. Her second attempt yielded the same response. Panicked, she called her husband.

As the father entered the room, the mother exclaimed, "I think our baby is deaf!"

The father was surprised at first.

"That is not true. You clearly breastfeed him and he is active. If you have been trying something and it hasn't worked, perhaps

Google has the answer," said the father.

"I have tried everything but I feel that the pediatrician could clear this up for us. He will be able to look at our son," said the mother.

The father walked over to the crib and picked up his son. He settled his son on his shoulder and patted him gently, humming the melody of his favorite blues track. Pretty soon, the baby started shifting in the father's arms. The father looked at the mother and smiled, not to show that she was wrong, but to indicate that everything was okay.

The mother sighs, but remains convinced that her son has a problem.

The couple visits the pediatrician, who says that their son is healthy and that there are no complications. Yet the mother remains unconvinced. A few days later, as she plays with the baby, it reacts to the sounds. She immediately feels relieved and lets out a joyful laugh.

The story gives us an insight into two different kinds of people; those who worry incessantly and those who don't let things beyond their control influence their lives too heavily. Many people might think that those who belong in the latter category are those who don't care about things. These people are indifferent to the events occurring around them.

That is not always the case. People who don't react immediately are those who have learned a fundamental truth about life. They know that they can only influence the things they can control and respond to things they cannot control. Which is why, they turn their attention towards actions. They are proactive. Life never hands over a silver platter laden with all the good stuff. You have to make the journey to the buffet table and along the way, you have to navigate dense crowds, slippery floors, fallings objects, and so many other obstacles.

Why is it important to understand that life has so many facets? Because most people cultivate negative thinking by focusing too much on the things that they can't control. And when they receive constant disappointment, they develop a pessimistic outlook, which is a deep pit that one cannot easily escape from.

How do you avoid falling into that pit? There are quite a few ways. The first thing you have to do is examine your habits. They might reveal quite a lot about you.

Discovering New Good Habits

Habits are powerful. They are truly influential.

To understand their power, one has to delve deeper into the mind, where we discover who – or what – is truly in control.

Think about this situation. You are headed home from work or any other point of origin. What matters is that you have taken the route home multiple times in your life so you know it like the back of your hand. One evening, you are taking this route when you realize that you are supposed to stop by the supermarket to purchase a carton of milk. As you plan out the evening, thoughts of the milk move on to the time you tried that incredible milkshake with your friends. Ruminations of your friends make you ponder about your weekend plans. You think it might be a fun idea to catch a movie at the local theatre or play a round of pool. That just reminded you, isn't it your friend's birthday next month? Perhaps you should get him something. If only your boss would give you your yearly bonus. But boy, you have so many projects to get done-

Wait a minute.

You have already reached home. But how? You don't remember the entire journey.

What you have experienced is a phenomenon called "highway hypnosis," which is like the distant cousin of line hypnosis. Your subconscious mind took control over your movements while your conscious self focused on the thoughts zipping through your brain. When you eventually reach your destination, your subconscious mind recognizes it and gives back the control to your conscious mind.

Even now, your subconscious mind is performing so many calculations as you read the words on this page. Your breathing, posture, blinking, heart rate, the way you are sitting, and so many other parts of your position are controlled by the subconscious mind.

So, you see, the subconscious mind is truly influential. What makes it powerful is the fact that you are never aware of its influence. It's a mental nudge and suggestion that goes mostly unnoticed. Everything is automatic. The confident feeling you get when you are wearing a suit or dress? That's your subconscious mind taking cues from your brain and the environment to create a response. The reason you feel pangs of sympathy for the homeless on the street? It's your subconscious mind pushing those thoughts into your brain.

Don't believe me? Then think of the last time that you saw someone who was disabled, homeless, or suffered from a form of debilitation and felt like that you wanted to help them. Do you remember each and every thought process that went through your head and forced you to arrive at the emotions you were feeling? Did you plan the course your mind would take in order to make you feel something? It felt like the emotion was just there when you felt it, didn't it?

This is your subconscious mind influencing you. In fact, the majority of emotions that we feel are spontaneous and encouraged by our subconscious mind.

But doesn't that make you think? If the subconscious mind does influence our emotions in such ways, who gave the directions to our subconscious to react in such a manner toward that particular scenario? When a barista gets our order wrong, why does our subconscious mind compel us to feel annoyed rather than be kind and forgiving?

That is dependent entirely on you.

When you act in a particular way, the subconscious mind records your actions and creates a mental program out of it. This program is used as a template for future actions. Your subconscious mind does this because you cannot handle each and every stimuli or situation that plays out in front of you. It would overwhelm your senses and overload your brain. Hence, your subconscious mind takes some of the workload while you can focus on other, more important things.

This method used by the subconscious – where a stimulus from the past affects your actions, thoughts, or feelings in the present – is called priming. And priming is a powerful tool used by your subconscious mind.

For example, if you have been ignoring your alarm clock to get extra sleep, your subconscious mind records that activity. Now every time you hear the alarm clock, you are capable of switching it off and going back to sleep. Sometimes, your subconscious mind throws in thoughts and images of how comfortable sleep really is just to entice you to return to bed. In some cases, you might even sleep past the alarm!

And that's where your bad habits come from.

The more you prime your subconscious mind to focus on bad habits, the more it incorporates them into your life.

Have you ever noticed people wake up in the morning and read motivational quotes? What they are doing is priming their brains, even though they don't realize it. By teaching the brain some motivational quotes, they are giving it a set of priming instructions. When they experience a challenging moment during their day, the subconscious mind goes back to the prime, which in this case are the motivational quotes, and uses them to add motivation into people's lives. When you start keeping your home clean, you feel clean because your subconscious mind has learned about how cleaning is good.

The Good Habits, The Bad Habits, and The Ugly Negativity

When you have good habits, you automatically start organizing your life, managing your time, and getting more focused.

You organize your life and make sure that things are in order in your house. You ensure that you do not delay tasks or work. There are schedules placed for various tasks. In little ways, you start removing chaos so that order can be ushered in.

The more order you create, the more efficiently you use your time. For example, by waking up early in the morning, you realize that you do not want to simply waste time, for that would be a bad habit. Rather, you go through the day's schedule, organize everything, get some exercise, and prepare a healthy breakfast. One by one, you eliminate your bad habits until you have very few of them.

You focus better as well. Once you start eliminating bad habits, you don't have unwanted thoughts distracting you. Additionally, you have completed your tasks on time. You now have the time to focus on other important things.

Each good habit you cultivate continues to pile up and bring more order into your life. Your subconscious, now inundated with all of these good habits, is slowly shooting positive messages into your brain. You become a better person.

But how is all of this related to negative thinking?

Let's take the example of waking up early in the morning. Your alarm rings but you shut it off and promptly sink your head into the pillow again. You don't want to deal with the day and it seems like you are well on your way to getting some extra shut-eye. This act convinces your subconscious that you would rather sleep than be active. Anytime you feel mentally exhausted, rather than take a walk or relax for a bit, you automatically start thinking of sleep. Over time, you notice that your body starts to feel sluggish. You end up believing that you're not a morning person. Because you did not have a good start to your day, this attitude carries forward into the rest of the tasks that you perform throughout the day. When you start seeing how your life revolves around bad mornings, lazy routines, and poor performances, during the rest of the day, you start to develop a negative outlook on life. Add to the fact that you have allowed so this all to happen and you have a recipe for negativity.

This becomes a cycle. You begin to attract more negativity, which teaches your subconscious mind to develop an unhealthy outlook on how to deal with situations. You begin to express your negative thinking in your actions. If someone accidentally bumped into you, rather than accept their apology, you respond with a scowl that could send people running for their dear lives. In such ways, you become a negative person. And the worst part? You don't realize the changes happening to you. Everything feels natural as the subconscious mind does not make these changes obvious. If you had used your conscious mind to make changes, then you would have been aware of them. But since your subconscious mind is the guide here, you think that things are the way they are because that's who you are.

This normality is harmful because it is easy to get used to. Think about this; when being lazy is normal, then why would anyone fight it? To make things worse, we also have to consider the psychological phenomenon of hindsight bias.

In Hindsight

Have you ever been in a situation where someone was telling you something and you exclaimed, "I was just about to do that"

You see, the brain wonderfully stores information. And edits them as well.

When you are in a situation where someone else beats you to the chase, your brain does not want to make you feel incompetent or slow. And so, as soon as the other person reveals the solution, your brain takes in the information, plants it in your memory, and erases parts of your old memory where you did not know the solution. This way, you feel as though you knew the solution all along. This phenomenon is known as hindsight bias and it is not always a bad thing.

You see, when you have too much related information in your brain, they all vie for control and attention. This leads to confusion, a jumbled-up memory, and unreliable information in your brain. And so, your brain deletes old memories so that you won't accidentally remember them. This system allows you to draw on the most relevant or recent memories that you have.

But where hindsight becomes harmful is when it starts working on your bad habits.

Once you start getting used to bad habits and your subconscious mind also starts believing in them, then your brain starts removing old memories. Once it does that, you might never have a proper recollection of the times you were active. You might remember the day you came first on the track team or scored 3 goals in soccer, since those are profound and impactful memories that the brain loves to preserve. But when it comes to daily routine, you might reflect back and think, "Well, I have always been this way. I don't think I have ever NOT acted in any way other than this way," even though you might have! You were an active person before. If you think hard enough, then you might find instances that showed what an energetic man or woman you were. However, your brain might have erased most of the memories so that you don't have contradicting thoughts about who you are.

Your subconscious mind, along with the phenomenon of hindsight bias, makes you feel like a completely different person.

All because you adopted a few bad habits.

The Difficulty of Creating Good Habits

When your subconscious mind starts believing something, it is quite difficult to change a habit.

Once you form habits, you might end up living with them for quite a while. Your subconscious mind gets used to this idea and the lifestyle you have created for yourself. When you eventually decide to change your lifestyle and incorporate good habits, your subconscious will do everything in its power to convince you otherwise.

At the same time, your brain loves convenience. Taking the longer or challenging route can be stressful. Your brain obviously wants to avoid stressful situations. It's part of the fight or flight instincts kicking in, convincing you that you are better off not trying to face danger. But life is never about easy answers and quick actions. Most of the things that we want in life are usually challenging to get. When you eventually decide to adopt good habits, your brain realizes that there is going to be a lot of work involved. You might have to sacrifice your entertainment, extra sleep, or other comforts that you have added to your life. This idea seems rather frightening to the brain. After all, why give up the good stuff or comfort to go for something else? This is why many people often make a New Year's resolution about hitting the gym, sign up for a membership, and never go back there again. They start their gym sessions in earnest and with much vigor. Eventually, their subconscious minds send them signals, ideas, and memories about all the things they could be doing instead, like binge-watching Netflix with a bowl of buttered popcorn. People might ignore these suggestions initially since they have developed an enthusiasm for the gym and the brain feeds off on that enthusiasm. Eventually, when the pain and discomfort begins to settle in, people start thinking about ways to decrease pain and experience more comfort. And that right there, is like giving permission to the subconscious mind to fill your thoughts with ideas of giving up.

Think about it this way. If you really want to make a difference in your life, why wait for a new year? What about the months you have right now? Are you going to throw them away simply because the beginning of the new year has a "starting point" quality to it?

The truth is that people who want to truly create good habits will choose to do it immediately, since they do not want to live with their bad habits anymore. They want to see changes happen as soon as possible, because they know that the more someone gets used to a habit, the more difficult it becomes to move away from it.

Sticking to Good Habits

Plunging yourself into numerous good habits at one time might add a lot of stress to your brain. You might experience a strong sense of withdrawal, where numerous bad habits are trying to lull you back to their domain, which might overwhelm you.

In order to change your lifestyle, here are some ways to inculcate good habits in your life.

Start Small

You might have known people who, all they want to do is try to attain results as fast as possible.

They start from zero gym sessions to five or six in a week, cut out meat entirely, meditate for 20 minutes every day, go jogging in the morning, and start heading to bed at 9 when they could barely stand 15 minutes in the gym before.

Try and understand your limits. Be aware of your mind's reactions. Each bad habit you are going to get rid of requires a tremendous amount of willpower. So, don't go through them like a bulldozer going through a small building without a proper plan. Start with one habit at a time.

Focus on going to the gym regularly and getting adequate sleep. Since these two are related, they will complement each other. Once you get used to the routine, you can add meditation to your list of new habits. If you find that you have little time to meditate in the morning, you can do it before you head to bed instead. You can adjust your routine so that it fits your schedule comfortably.

For any good habit you want to incorporate into your life, start small and make sure that you get used to one before moving on to the other.

Become Hooked on Good Habits

Have you ever noticed how you do not like to get rid of the things you have invested a lot of time and effort into?

Pick up a calendar. Each day you spend perfecting your habits receives an X on the calendar. Over time, you will notice that your calendar is covered with lots of X marks. When you notice this, you will realize that you have put in so much effort into your new habit already. It would be a shame to give it up now. That motivates you to continue with your work even more.

Planning to jog every morning? Keep marking your activity on the calendar until you become hooked.

You might start out by refusing to let go of your bad habits. It might seem that the only reason you are holding on to them is sheer stubbornness. Over time, when you become used to the good habits, that's when an old psychological phenomenon friend comes to pay you a visit; hindsight bias.

You might have started believing in your good habits because you don't want to waste your time and effort, but you will eventually start believing that you wanted to change your bad habits into good because you wanted to. Your brain will start erasing memories of you feeling compelled to change your bad habits. All you might remember is that you started working on your good habits and through sheer determination, you ended up succeeding in incorporating them into your life.

And that is not a bad thing. Why continue to believe that you felt forced to do something? You have good habits now after all. It does not matter how you got here.

Have Clear Goals

When you start creating goals with vague intentions, then you are more than likely not going to follow through because you are not entirely certain how you want to achieve your goals. Here are some examples:

- I am going to go to the gym three times a week.
- I am going to sleep as early as possible and wake up at dawn.
- I will have breakfast in the morning.

Why are the above goals vague? They don't have a plan of action. What does "sleep as early as possible" mean? It could be

8 pm or it could be 6 pm. You could sleep at 8 pm one day and then at 11 pm the next day and still consider it early.

The best way to create new habits is by having a plan of action.

- Form implementation intentions, where you create a series of if/then conditions. For example, "If I wake up early in the morning, then I will do cardio and 10 pushups."
- Once you create the above condition, stack your habits. For example, before I head to the gym in the morning, I am going to get 8 hours of sleep where I head to bed by 9 pm.
- Start scheduling. Once you have a rough outline, create a schedule in your calendar where you note down the time that you are going to head to bed, when you are going to the gym, and the duration you are going to spend there. When you have your plans distilled to accurate timings, you won't continue to rely on wiggle room to allow you to make the endeavor easier.

Make it a Rewarding Experience

Some people save rewards for big milestones. The problem with that is that it might take a while for them to reach those milestones.

If you don't reward yourself frequently, then you are going to feel like the journey is not worth it. Every step that you take in your journey is a win, no matter how small it is. For example, making sure that you wake up in the morning to head to the gym is a win. After all, people actively avoid waking up early. You pushing through the fog of sleep and putting your body through a fitness regime is a success in itself.

At the same time, you should not reward yourself too often or it loses its meaning. Your rewarding technique has to be realistic, but motivating.

The best way to do this is to think of the goal you would like to achieve. Then break up that goal into smaller parts. For example, let's say you are aiming for killer abs. You know that you might achieve your ideal body after months of hard work. Ideally, your reward schedule should be done on a weekly basis. This means that if you successfully complete a week's worth of exercise, then you are eligible for a reward. This way, you not only space out the reward at comfortable intervals, but you keep yourself motivated.

Let's look at another example. Imagine that you have decided to wake up at 4 am every day. Currently, you wake up at 8 am and start your day with a hot latte at about 9 am. You are hoping to change that. For your new schedule, you are not going to have your latte unless you have woken up at 4 am for three consecutive days. You are going to stick to black coffee for two days and have your latte on the third day. If you break your routine at any point, then the cycle restarts.

Each cycle is a chance to reinforce your habit. As you continue to reward yourself, you will continue to reinforce the habit. Eventually, it has become a part of your life and your brain will recognize this as well. As for the rest, you can leave it to hindsight bias to make you feel like you were always interested in the habit.

Redesign Your Environment

Remember that we discussed how when people read motivational quotes in the morning, they are priming themselves for the rest of the day? You can do that in this section as well as it is extremely effective in motivating you.

Let's take another example. If you have seen some office spaces (or perhaps your boss's office), then you might notice the presence of plants, paint on the wall, or other forms of decor. The aim of these features is to create an environment that boasts a certain personality. People with plants on their desk or in their offices are aiming for a calm and composed personality, where they are in control of their emotions. Those who have pictures of family or friends on their desk are revealing their values and what matters to them. Each of these objects is a mental reminder.

In a similar manner, surround yourself with items and paraphernalia that supports your habits. If you are planning to start working out regularly at the gym, put up motivational quotes by big muscled men or women who have bodies that look like they could deflect bullets. Keep your exercise gear close to you. You might even have a certain diet regime. If that diet involves meal preparation, then prepare these meals in advance and keep them in the refrigerator to have them ready for your day. All of these little steps contribute towards a mental attitude that will help you achieve your goals.

Create a space that motivates you and supports your work or habits.

Positive Habits Require Positive Thinking

You are about to go on a vacation to Bali. Here are a few situations that I would like to present to you. See if you like any of them.

- You are an adventurer. You love taking risks. It's all about the adrenaline and facing your fears. You enjoy extreme sports. However, I tell you that all you get to do on your vacation is stay in your hotel and relax.
- You are an explorer. You love to see the sights, people, food, and events of the city you visit. To you, the excitement of discovery comes before everything else. I tell you that you are only allowed to visit a restaurant frequented by tourists and nothing else. And maybe a shopping mall.
- You enjoy relaxation. The main purpose of your vacation is to sit back, remove your footwear, and sip on that cocktail while enjoying a lovely book. But guess what? I

wake you up at 5 am and tell you that we are going rock climbing!

Would you really enjoy your vacation in any of the three scenarios? Would you have positive emotions when thinking about your trip? In fact, you might not even listen to what I have to say and do what you came to do.

If you do not like something, chances are that you are going to find a way to avoid it. It might happen immediately or it might happen eventually. The same goes with your habits as well. All of the above steps mentioned under "Sticking to Good Habits" try to encourage you to do so. But they will need the assistance of your positive mindset.

Now the important question is; just how do you develop this mindset?

The Power of Positive Thinking

You might think that any subject related to "positive thinking" might be covered mostly by psychologists or life coaches. You might have never thought that the medical community might actually start looking into the topic. But they did, and the results are pretty surprising. According to Mayo Clinic (Mayo Clinic Staff, n.d.), positive thinking provides you with many benefits including:

- Lower rates of depression

- Longer life
- Lower stress levels
- Improved cardiovascular health
- Improved coping skills during times of stress

Of course, a lot of people might say, "How is cardiovascular health involved in all of this?"

Your cardiovascular health depends on a lot of factors. It depends on your diet, the hours of sleep you get, the degree of stress you face, and more. Negative thoughts fuel negative emotions, which in turn causes stress to arise easily in your brain. For example, you are in bad traffic and your thinking is already in a negative state. You are already adding stress to your brain because your thoughts keep conjuring ideas and memories that trigger stress. Because of that, you might not be able to deal with the traffic well. This means more stress. Which in turn means that you exacerbate your negative emotions. And eventually, you have a cycle.

When your body is under a lot of stress, it increases cholesterol and blood pressure levels. That in turn affects your heart.

Positive thinking is not just essential for good mental health, but contributes to good physical health as well.

How exactly can we create a positive mindset? Let us examine some of the ways.

Tip #1: Start Your Day with Affirmations

The tone you adopt in the morning can dictate how the rest of the day might proceed. Why not set a positive tone for yourself? In fact, have you ever had an experience where you woke up in a state of panic, wondering if you forgot to complete an important task or if you are late for something, only to realize that nothing has happened and it was just your nerves? Or have you woken up once in such a state of stress that you could not even finish the coffee you made for yourself? All of these situations have occurred because when you start your day poorly, the emotions trickle over to the next day. Eventually, you are living in a constant state of stress and negativity. Affirmations are simple phrases that help you focus on positive emotions. Every time you wake up, start the day with phrases like:

- Today, I shall face my day with courage and positivity.
- Today might be challenging, but so is any day of the week. I shall not let these challenges change my perspective of the world and create negativity.
- I am an incredible person and despite today's events, I will not look down on myself.
- Today is going to be a good day.
- I'm going to be awesome and nothing is going to convince me otherwise!

You can always create your own positive affirmations depending on the situation.

Tip #2: Think About the Good Things, No Matter How Small They Are

Don't wait for a big moment to occur in your life. Look at every small event as another positive contribution. Here is the reality of life: no matter how much you want to avoid obstacles, you are going to encounter them every day. Each obstacle is something that has the potential to add to a whole pile of negative things. Eventually, you will feel that your life has too much negativity in it. What you are experiencing is small things that have accumulated to become something intimidating.

The same rule applies with the positive things in your life as well. Keep collecting them, no matter how little they seem. Eventually, the number of positive things will add up to become a dominating presence in your life.

Tip #3: Crank Up Your Humor

Don't let the dark situations get you down. Teach yourself to see the humor in things. Remind yourself that the situation you are in is going to get better eventually. After all, life goes on. Regardless of what happens to whom, life is a continuous ticking clock. So, make a joke out of the things that have happened to you and move on.

Tip #4: Failures Are Lessons

Success finds those people who are not brooding over their failures, but are finding ways to move past them. But the only way that can happen is if they choose to learn from their failures.

You too should approach your failures with tact and wisdom. Let your failures teach you a lesson; do not let them define your life. Bill Gates is defined by the success of Microsoft because he let that be the focus of his attention. If he had let his failures define him, then he would be in a different position rather than on the Forbes list of billionaires.

Tip #5: Watch Out for Negative Self-Talk

It's not unusual for people to berate themselves when they commit an error. How many times have you thought "I shouldn't have done it. I was going to fail anyway" when you tried something and didn't succeed at it? Or you might have thought one of these critical thoughts:

- Why do I even bother with such things anyway?
- What am I doing? I should have just stuck to what I know.
- If only I hadn't tried something new, this wouldn't have happened.

Every time you create a negative statement about yourself, you are forcing your brain to think in a particular manner. And we don't need to go into the details of how your subconscious is going to latch on to those negative thoughts and run with them.

So, what should you do if you are faced with negative self-evaluations? You turn them into positive ones.

Let's say that you tried to do something and it failed. Rather than thinking:

- I shouldn't have tried. This is what happens when you don't stick to what you do.

Think of it this way:

- So that's what happens if I do it this way! Interesting! I'll remember this and make sure I don't do it this way in the future. Or even if I do, I will plan better. Let's look at my other options.

Notice the difference? In the second response, you acknowledge that a mistake has been made. But you see it in a positive light. You allow it to teach you rather than defeat you. Make sure that you are not denying the fact that you have made a mistake. Denial has its consequences.

What is so bad about denial, you ask?

A lot.

One of the things that denial prevents you from doing is seeking help. We are not all perfect. Sometimes, we need help in our endeavors. That does not mean that we are weak or unskilled. It just means that we might need an extra pair of hands (or more) to help us with our project.

Denial also prevents us from acknowledging problems. If you feel that there are no problems, even when there are, then you won't learn to grow or deal with them. Eventually, those problems worsen and affect your life immensely at a later time.

There are two things you can do with a problem.

You can choose to face it and learn to handle it. Or you can choose to ignore it, and watch it dismantle things in your life.

Among the two options, the ideal choice is obvious.

Focus on the Present

People often misunderstand this advice. They think that by being focused on the present, they have to be aware of every ticking minute that passes by.

That's not true at all. The idea of being in the present – or practicing mindfulness as people like to say – is that you don't let your mind wander toward things of the past or events of the future. The reason for this is that the things of the past have already occurred and there is nothing you can do to change that. But, what about the things that are yet to happen? Use the steps below:

- Step 1: Can you deal with the situation? If yes, move on to Step 2, else move on to Step 5.

- Step 2: Have you already thought of ways to deal with the situation? If yes, move on to Step 5, else move on to Step 3
- Step 3: Can you come up with recommendations, ideas, or solutions to deal with the situation? If you yes, move on to step 4, else go to Step 5.
- Step 4: Do you have a plan of action? If yes, then move to Step 5, else create a plan of action and move to Step 5.
- Step 5: Continue with your day and bring your mind back to the present.

When you allow the past or present to occupy too much of your time in the present, then you might not perform well or achieve much in the present.

Have a Positive Circle of Friends

Let me meet your friends and I can tell you what your future looks like. You might have heard that phrase repeated often. And for good reason. Since it does bear some truth.

When you surround yourself with friends who are positive influences in your life, you in turn improve your positivity.

Take this study conducted by Harvard psychologists as an example (Fowler & Christakis, 2008). The study was conducted over a period of 20 years and the results showed that happiness is greatly influenced by your social circles. In other words, you might very well be the company you keep.

When you surround yourself with positive people, their positivity seeps into your life. You become a sponge, absorbing their attitudes and eventually adding certain quirks to your own personality.

Have friends who support you and accept you for who you are.

Hence, surround yourself with people who help you increase the positivity in your life.

Additionally, you can also find people who can act as your mentors. It could be your parents, siblings, friends, or even grandparents. Being in the company of positive people will allow you to learn from their attitudes. They might even be able to share some of their worldly wisdom with you.

Effects of Positivity on Health

Having upsetting thoughts in your mind can be rather frustrating. Sometimes, they could lead to depression and you are often left wondering if you are getting upsetting thoughts because of your depression or if you are depressed because of your sad thoughts. You will then be left trying to create some kind of connection between the two when in reality, you should be focused on something else.

Your negative thoughts.

Remember how we talked about the subconscious mind reacting to the way we think and act in every day life? When our minds are filled with negative thoughts, then our subconscious begins to create emotions to deal with them. If your negative thoughts are frustrating, then your subconscious will react with anger. If they are sentimental, then you might be sad, and so on.

Eventually, when you cannot deal with the negativity much more, you become depressed. And that causes its own set of problems.

- People who have depression might experience a drastic shift in their appetite, which might cause them to lose or gain a lot of weight. Depression has also been tied to other conditions such as diabetes and heart disease.
- Depression has also been linked to chronic pain. And it gets worse. When the pain worsens, it also affects your levels of depression. Eventually, you have a cycle of pain and depression (Coryell, 2018).
- Inflammation is a natural reaction by the body. It is useful to prevent infections and occurs when your body receives external damage or injuries. Your inflammation process helps the immune system deal with the damage. But the process of inflammation is accompanied by a high fight-or-flight response. The longer the fight-or-flight response, the more stress your body has to deal with. This is why, when the danger has passed, your

body automatically works to calm you down. However, when you are depressed, you can experience inflammation in the body (E. Leonard, 2010). This means that your body is in a state of stress when there is no problem for it to face. The longer your state of depression, the longer the state of stress, which eventually begins to affect your cardiovascular health and your digestive system.

- Negative thoughts also cause sleeping problems. When this happens, you end up becoming more exhausted, leading to a degradation in mental and physical health. Additionally, you might find yourself unable to deal with the situations you come across every day and have poor judgement. Your memory might become faulty since the lack of mental energy might force your brain to reject new information.

When you examine negative thoughts as a whole, they are the cause for serious mental and physical health problems. Many times, you wouldn't necessarily think about negative thoughts as the reason for so many health problems. But if you examine your life and notice that you have negative thoughts on a consistent basis, then perhaps it is time to deal with them to prevent your health from getting worse than it already might be.

Becoming Happier

Everyone wants to be happy. Yet, many people don't know how. Some believe that by having more possessions, they will definitely find something fulfilling. Don't get me wrong, you are allowed to treat yourself whenever you can. But those are not the only ways you can add happiness to your life. And they might definitely not be long-lasting, since you might end up looking for the next best thing to buy.

How do you find lasting happiness?

Let us look at some ways.

Happiness Tip #1: Find Ways to Feel Better About Yourself

Think of your favorite car, mobile device, or any other item. It could be your favorite clothing brand or restaurant.

Now think of all the things you love about that brand, place, or object. Next, imagine someone saying that what you like is a terrible option. What would you say to them? Would you simply accept their feedback or would you actually try and explain to them why your choice is actually great?

If you can find the good in objects, places, and situations, then why can't you find positive traits in yourself? Put yourself in the same position as the things that you love. What are some positive points about yourself that you can think about? Imagine someone pointing out your faults. How would you show them that despite your faults, you are an individual with good traits as well?

When you start evaluating in such a manner, you might find out that there are more reasons to be you than people know. You are something special, just like the many things you admire in your life. Even if people say something negative about something you like, you should be ready with a rebuttal.

You deserve the same defense as well. You need to have a sense of brand loyalty towards yourself; the biggest brand in your life.

Happiness Tip #2: Create Balance

If you have ever worked with accounting, then you might be familiar with the balance sheet you have to tally. The assets should always be equal to the liabilities, which is the fundamental rule of a double-entry bookkeeping system.

Your life is a series of checks and balances. Your life story is a giant book of accounts. Your assets are all the achievements you have made, the things you are proud of, your goals and dreams, and your positive emotions.

Your liabilities are all the negative ideas, failures, and anything else that you can add in here that you aren't proud of. Hence, for every liability, you need to have an asset. Your failures should be met with lessons learned from those failures or successes. Your negative emotions should be met with an equal surge of positive emotions.

Most importantly, your work should be paired with a life outside of work.

Having a work-life balance is crucial. Don't put yourself in a position where you are going to suffer from repeated burnouts. That does not constitute a healthy life. If you feel that you have no choice but to go through a rather long and difficult period at work, then make sure that you have planned a holiday to recuperate from that period.

Do not go from one task to another. Make sure that you are taking breaks for yourself.

Happiness Tip #3: Make Positive Memories

Memories are powerful. They not only remind us about certain periods in our lives, but also influence our subconscious mind.

Which is why, take your time to make as many positive memories as possible. These memories do not have to be big. Start small. Spend time with your family. Take your friends out for a drink. Sit back and watch a fun movie. Every small action adds up to a bigger action. It's like a snowball effect; you will eventually have one giant snowball of positive memories.

Happiness Tip #4: Be Kind and Generous

There is plenty of research that explains the link between kindness and happiness (Cohut, 2017).

You don't have to donate a lot of money or make a big contribution in some way to show that you are a kind person. Demonstrate it in little ways. Treat the strangers you meet, especially people who work in the service industry like waiters and receptionists, with kindness and respect. Send a smile someone's way. Greet people with genuine warmth. Make a child smile. Feed the local stray cats. There are so many ways you can express your kindness and generosity.

This also relates to the previous point. The more kindness you show, the more good memories you accumulate. Eventually, you start seeing yourself in a new light. Did someone really say that you were a terrible person? How can that be? In fact, the next time someone comments on your negative qualities, you will have enough mental strength to ignore them. That's because you truly know that you are not what people make you out to be.

Happiness Tip #5: Make Offline Connections

Don't think that the only way you can connect with people is through the virtual world of social media. Step out and make some genuine connections. Meeting people in real life is much more rewarding than simply trying to send them a message online.

Psychologists have shown that Facebook and other social media platforms have a negative impact on our happiness (Davis, 2017). Why? Because we are not in the presence of the other person to see their reactions. When you sit face-to-face with someone, you are able to see their emotions visibly reflected in their reactions and body language. Your mirror neurons, responsible for empathy, are able to reflect this in your own reactions. When you are sitting in front of a computer screen, all you see is a series of digits and images. Your brain cannot process that in the same way.

Happiness Tip #6: Spend Smart

Having money in your pockets is definitely a bonus. Which is why, you should avoid spending more than you are able to. Always make sure that you have money for emergencies and other important aspects in your life. This does not mean that you should not spend on the things that you want. But create a budget if you find yourself short on money repeatedly.

Make sure that when you are creating your budget, you allot a sum of money for the essential components of your life, such as bills, expenses, any debts you have to pay, and for medical or personal emergencies. If you are planning a holiday, retirement, or getting a brand-new car, make sure that you have a separate savings account for that. Once you have accounted for everything, you can use what you have left for spending. When you take careful account of your money, you are going to be much wiser about where you spend it.

Happiness Tip #7: Engage with Negativity

It's good that you are going to focus on the positive. But that does not mean that you simply ignore the negativity. Let's face it; life is not going to take it easy on you just because you took on a positive outlook. So, don't wait for the negatives to pile up. Deal with them immediately.

Remember to create an armor against negativity. When you acknowledge the negativity in your life, then know how to deal with it. Think of it like your immune system that identifies viruses and infections and is able to better deal with them in the future. When you face negative thinking, you understand it better and create a mental immune system.

Happiness Tip #8: Identify and Live Your Values

Try and set aside some time to explore your values. You might be surprised by the fact that you might already have had some positive values in your life, but because of all the negativity, you were not able to hold on to them.

Happiness Tip #9: Set Achievable Goals

Make your life productive. Start creating goals that you would like to achieve. Then break down those goals into smaller objectives. For example, let us say that you are planning to learn how to cook. Your end goal is to master cooking, but your individual objectives could be much smaller. You could plan your first objective to try preparing your first successful dish. Then you could move on to desserts, and so on.

Happiness Tip #10: Speak Up

Do not always hold back your opinions. If something makes you feel uncomfortable or you do not agree with something, speak up. Feel free to express yourself. Reality is not a vacuum that you experience with your eyes like a computer, defining everything as a series of 1s and 0s. It is actually a complex construct that is made up of moments and experiences that impact the way you think and feel. Make sure you are not sacrificing what you believe in for someone else's beliefs.

Happiness Tip #11: Be Accountable

Take charge of your life. It is more rewarding than simply letting things take their own course. When you feel accountable for your actions, you begin to plan them out better. You are less likely to believe that you can't do anything about your goals and more likely to start planning to achieve them. You will disregard those things that you cannot control and focus on what is within your control.

Conclusion

People often think that creating a positive frame of mind is rather easy. But in today's busy world, it might not be as easy as they originally thought.

However, I think that all good habits are like learning a new skill. You might find it difficult to learn the skill but that is only because you have been used to a certain lifestyle. Think about it this way; you are used to living with certain bad habits for a long time, even decades for some. Trying to change them in a matter of a few days is going to be truly challenging. Which is why you should focus on using the techniques provided in this book over time. You don't have to start changing all your habits in one go. You might add a lot of unneeded stress in your life this way. While the road ahead might be long, I can say that it will be truly rewarding.

Here is something you could focus on. Try creating a mental picture. In this mental picture, imagine how you are going to be like when you have adopted the positive thinking techniques and good habits in this book. Think about the changes you are going to make in your life. Try and imagine what that person would be doing, how productive he or she is going to be, and how much improvement he or she is going to bring to his or her life. Watch as the person becomes a better, confident, and positive individual. You can see the person form positive relationships and focus on constantly improving life. That person has learned to live life to the fullest.

Now imagine the same person without all the good habits and positivity mentioned in this book. Think about the fact that the person might just return to the same routine, the same detrimental thought patterns and self-destructive behavior. That person has no purpose in life and fails to see anything positive. Looking at that person's life is like looking at a painting with many shades of gray; it's depressing and devoid of vibrancy.

Think about who you want to be.

Keep that goal in your mind as you tackle the recommendations and advice provided in this book.

The journey to a good life is paved with many challenges. But those challenges show you the kind of person you are. In fact, when you reach your destination, you might look back and say, "Well, that wasn't so bad now, was it?"

Think about a time when you had experienced a challenge and you were nervous. However, if you were asked to recall the same incident right now, you might talk about it as though it was a story. The entire experience might not bother you and you might scoff at the idea that you were so worried back then.

You see, things are always intimidating when they are up close. It is only when they are viewed from a distance that they seem less frightening. This is why, when we look back at many incidents in our past, we view them from a distance. The only difference being that it's not a physical distance, but the distance of time. Nonetheless, it is a place far away from the original experience.

If you ever feel intimidated by how challenging some things might turn out to be, then take a step back. Examine the broader view of the situation. Think about its impact on your future and who you are going to be. That is the main purpose of the visualization technique I asked you to do earlier. It helps you to think about distances, where you try to position yourself in the future, quite far from the situation in the present. It allows you to step away from the challenge.

When you are able to examine the whole picture, you might understand just what you should do.

I also advise you to never worry too much about what others might think. You are on a path to create meaningful changes in your life. You don't have to involve anyone who does not have to be part of the change. It is almost like those times you go to the gym and feel suddenly so self-conscious that you just want to pack up and leave. But there is no need for that. Chances are that everyone in the gym is there to achieve a certain goal. And if they are not encouraging or helping you achieve your goals, then why bother worrying about them? After all, aren't we talking about eliminating the negative here?

So, head out and make a world of change. Do not stop for anything. Make yourself the center of your journey.

It is time to bring more positivity into your life.

References

Blaszczak-Boxe, A. (2017, May 3). Don't worry if you're a worrier . . . It could be good for you. *LiveScience*. Retrieved from www.livescience.com/58951-why-worrying-can-be-good-for-you.html

Bloom, L. & Bloom, C. (2017, February 27). Re-setting your happiness set point: Part 1. *HuffPost*. Retrieved from huffpost.com/entry/re-setting-your-happiness-set-point-part-1_b_58b45d1e4b02f3f81e44a6e

Brownstein, J. (2011, July 26). Planning 'worry time' may help ease anxiety. *LiveScience*. Retrieved from livescience.com/15233-planning-worry-time-ease-anxiety.html

Cappuccio, F. P., Taggart, F. M., Kandala, N. B., Currie, A., Peile, E., Stranges, S., & Miller, M. A. (2008). Meta-analysis of short sleep duration and obesity in children and adults. Sleep, 31(5), 619–626. doi:10.1093/sleep/31.5.619

Colier, N. (2019, April 15). Negative thinking: A dangerous addiction. *Psychology Today*. Retrieved from psychologytoday.com/us/blog/inviting-monkey-tea/201904/negative-thinking-dangerous-addiction

Coryell, W. (2018). Depressive Disorders - Psychiatric Disorders - MSD Manual Professional Edition. Retrieved 14 October 2019, from https://www.msdmanuals.com/en-gb/professional/psychiatric-disorders/mood-disorders/depressive-disorders

Davis, T. (2017). Is Facebook Bad for You?. Retrieved 14 October 2019, from https://www.psychologytoday.com/intl/blog/click-here-happiness/201711/is-facebook-bad-you

E. Leonard, B. (2010). The Concept of Depression as a Dysfunction of the Immune System. Current Immunology Reviews, 6(3), 205-212. doi: 10.2174/157339510791823835

Fight-Flight-Freeze. (n.d.). *Anxiety Canada*. Retrieved from anxietycanada.com/articles/fight-flight-freeze

Fonken, L., Workman, J., Walton, J., Weil, Z., Morris, J., Haim, A., & Nelson, R. (2010). Light at night increases body mass by shifting the time of food intake. Proceedings Of The National Academy Of Sciences, 107(43), 18664-18669. doi: 10.1073/pnas.1008734107

Fowler, J., & Christakis, N. (2008). Dynamic spread of happiness in a large social network: longitudinal analysis over 20 years in the Framingham Heart Study. BMJ, 337(dec04 2), a2338-a2338. doi: 10.1136/bmj.a2338

Grohol, J.M. (2018, October 8). What is catastrophizing? *PsychCentral*. Retrieved from https://psychcentral.com/lib/what-is-catastrophizing/

Hardy, B. (2018, June 9). To have what you want, you must give up what's holding you back. *Medium.com*. Retrieved from www.medium.com/the-mission/to-have-what-you-want-you-must-give-up-whats-holding-you-back

Hoffman, A. (2015, June 26). Can negative thinking make you sick? *Health.com*. Retrieved from health.com/heart-disease/can-negative-thinking-make-you-sick

Issa, F., & Sullivan, C. (1982). Alcohol, snoring and sleep apnea. Journal Of Neurology, Neurosurgery & Psychiatry, 45(4), 353-359. doi: 10.1136/jnnp.45.4.353

Laroche, Loretta. (2008). *Relax, You May Only Have a Few Minutes Left: Using the Power of Humor to Overcome Stress in Your Life and Work.* Carlsbad, CA: Hay House, Inc.

Mah, C. D., Mah, K. E., Kezirian, E. J., & Dement, W. C. (2011). The effects of sleep extension on the athletic performance of collegiate basketball players. Sleep, 34(7), 943–950. doi:10.5665/SLEEP.1132

Montenegro, R. (2015, March 9). People who constantly complain are harmful to your health. *Big Think*. Retrieved from https://bigthink.com/mind-brain/constant-complaining

Ressler, K. J. (2010). Amygdala activity, fear, and anxiety: Modulation by stress. *Biological Psychiatry, 67*(12), 1117-1119

Vitelli, R. (2013, November 18). Media exposure and the "perfect" body. *Psychology Today*. Retrieved from psychologytoday.com/us/blog/media-spotlight/201311/media-exposure-and-the-perfect-body

Made in United States
Orlando, FL
22 September 2023